High Tea at a Low Table

Stories from an Irish Childhood

ANGELA PATTEN

Also by Angela Patten:

Reliquaries

Still Listening

High Tea at a Low Table

Stories from an Irish Childhood

ANGELA PATTEN

Published by

WIND RIDGE BOOKS of vermont

Shelburne, Vermont 05482

High Tea at a Low Table, Stories from an Irish Childhood
Copyright 2013 by Angela Patten

All rights reserved. No part of this book may be used or reproduced in any manner whatsoever without written permission except in the case of brief quotations embodied in critical articles and reviews.

Cover and book design by Laurie Thomas
Back cover photo of author by Craig Thomas

ISBN: 978-1-935922-28-5
Library of Congress: 2013913640

Published by Wind Ridge Books of Vermont
PO Box 636
Shelburne, VT 05482

Printed in the United States of America

Dedication

For Daniel, and for my siblings John, Mary and Susan who will, no doubt, have their own versions of the story. And for my son Zak, as always.

Contents

Acknowlegements ix
Chapter One 3
Chapter Two 5
Chapter Three 12
Chapter Four 14
Chapter Five 17
Chapter Six 23
Chapter Seven 25
Chapter Eight 35
Chapter Nine 39
Chapter Ten 43
Chapter Eleven 48
Chapter Twelve 51
Chapter Thirteen 56
Chapter Fourteen 59
Chapter Fifteen 61
Chapter Sixteen 63
Chapter Seventeen 68
Chapter Eighteen 71
Chapter Nineteen 73
Chapter Twenty 75
Chapter Twenty-One 79
Chapter Twenty-Two 82
Chapter Twenty-Three 87
Chapter Twenty-Four 90
Chapter Twenty-Five 94

Chapter Twenty-Six	97
Chapter Twenty-Seven	100
Chapter Twenty-Eight	103
Chapter Twenty-Nine	106
Chapter Thirty	109
Chapter Thirty-One	113
Chapter Thirty-Two	115
Epilogue	117

Acknowlegements

Special thanks to my brother John Goggins, our family genealogist, for his research and encouragement; to Margaret Edwards for her editorial insights; to Gail Rosenberg for her wit, humor, and encouragement during the writing process; to Sue Burton and Baron Wormser who read the manuscript in its early stages; to my editor Lin Stone for shepherding this book to publication; and most of all to my husband Daniel Lusk who provided morning coffee and conversation, and a safe harbor in which to write.

"The world is made up of stories, not atoms."
—*Muriel Rukeyser*

Chapter One

On a sunny February afternoon in 1984, I drove into the parking lot at the University of Vermont in Burlington, found a parking space, and switched off the ignition. Then I held my breath, waiting for the explosion. The Subaru was a real lemon, in color and condition. I bought it for $500 when I left my marriage and moved into an apartment on my own. I was clueless about cars and terrified of driving but I had to be able to pick up my son and deliver him to school. I didn't realize I would need to pour quarts of oil into the engine every day and I cracked the block in my first month of ownership. I had to borrow another $500 to get it fixed but the car still had a few disturbing quirks. "For an intelligent girl, you can be very foolish," my mother would have said, clucking her tongue in disapproval. But she was far away in Dublin and blissfully ignorant about my troubles. I put the thought out of my head and reflected instead on the Romantic Poetry class I had just attended and the Anthropology exam scheduled for next day. I was a full-time English major, putting myself through college with the help of a half-time secretarial job in The Center for Developmental Disabilities. As a thirty-two-year-old single mother in school with nineteen-year-olds, I felt somewhat developmentally delayed myself. My son moved unhappily back and forth between me and his Dad, spending exactly half his week with each parent. It was a fractured existence but I clung to my poetry and literature studies like a drowning sailor to a spar, not sure whether to cry for help or just keep paddling.

I was walking toward the rear of the building when I noticed a young man coming toward me. I registered brown hair, slight build, faded plaid shirt. He repeatedly glanced right and left as he approached. Perhaps he's lost or has car trouble, I thought, preparing to offer assistance in my friendly Irish way. "Get back in the car," he hissed. I stared at him, hardly able to believe my ears. I looked around quickly, noticing how quiet the usually crowded parking lot was—not a soul in sight. I was about to run in the opposite direction when the man took a gun from his pocket and pointed it at me. It was a small handgun that fit snugly in his palm. The steel barrel caught the sunlight and shone like a jewel. What was I to do? This wasn't a story I had read in a book. It was the real world cutting in, as if the radio of my thoughts had gone suddenly dead.

The weapon created an immediate intimacy between us. There was something obscene about its sudden intrusion. I felt the rest of the world, the parking lot full of snow-dusted cars, and the red-brick office building gilded in the pale light of the afternoon, fall away under my feet. My head felt light, as if detached from the rest of my body. I began to fumble in my bag for the car-key. "Don't make me use this," the man said in a shaky voice. "Okay, okay. Take it easy," I managed to mumble. I could tell by his face that he was serious. Suddenly there was no question about what I should do. We both understood the simple, universal language of violence. I got back in the car on the passenger side. He took my keys and started the engine. As we drove down the street, I kept seeing people I knew, but they were oblivious to me. We turned the corner onto Colchester Avenue and I thought about jumping out at the traffic lights. "Lock that door," the man barked suddenly. I obeyed, sinking back into my seat.

Chapter Two

It was far from guns and kidnappers I was reared, as my father might have said. I grew up during the 1950s and '60s in Sallynoggin, a working-class neighborhood about seven miles south of Dublin City. This was an era in which the ragman, the slopman, and the coalman still came to our doorsteps with horses and carts, and Mr. Byrne, the milkman, arrived on his bicycle to ladle loose milk from a tilley-can. In this pre-technological world, stories were our entertainment and our sustenance. The nuns at school terrorized us with tales of leprosy and the foreign missions, black babies desperately in need of baptism, and sudden appearances by celestial beings. The radio brought plays, sponsored programs, and serialized stories for children. There were true stories too, like the assault by a priest that cost my father his eye, my narrow escape from being sent to an orphanage, and my first cousin's discovery that the woman he had always called "Aunt Kathleen" was really his mother. Over it all lay my mother's mellifluous but incessant talking that formed the foundation of my literary education.

My mother and her relations were all great talkers. If they had been runners, they could have competed at the marathon level. My father, on the other hand, came from silent country people and he was always warning us not to be talking to strangers. Country people, my mother explained, were moody and secretive. "They're too quiet and they never tell you about their affairs," she said of our rural relations, "but they're nosey enough to find out everything about you."

Mother, or Mammy, was born Annie Elizabeth Mary Swords in 1913, the daughter of a sailor from the Northside of Dublin and a seamstress from the County Wicklow. She grew up in Glasthule, Dublin, cheek-by-jowl with countless relations and innumerable neighbors, a stone's throw from the seaside, the shops, the red-brick Harold National School that she attended until the age of thirteen, and Glasthule Church where she married my father in 1948. Her relations were all sailors, and we loved her stories of their adventures on the high seas with the British Navy and the descriptions of the silk fans, lace shawls and other exotic gifts they brought back from foreign parts.

Dad, on the other hand, was a "culchie," born in 1918 in Addinstown, County Meath. He grew up in a small, whitewashed house on one acre of land. His father had been born in the house next door and, although his five brothers emigrated to America, the move from one house to another was the only one our grandfather made for the rest of his life.

These fundamental differences formed the basis of our identity as children. We were Irish, we were Catholic, we were poor, and our parents were as different as chalk and cheese.

I grew up among Mammy's jovial Dublin relations in a world that was filled with sounds—harsh, sweet and various. There were the murmured prayers of the priests at mass, the hymn-singing of nuns at school, the shouts of children on the street, the rasping lilt of paperboys, the rumble of double-decker buses, the metrical chuffing of steam-trains, and the rhythm of Dad's infectious fiddle playing. But the world came in at my ear most of all through Mammy's melodious voice as she recited poems and platitudes, dispensed advice, sang Irish songs, retold the novels she read at night, and entertained us with the story of her life as she cooked and cleaned and cared for us.

I was a shy, fearful, bookish child and it was a long time before I discovered my own voice, still longer before I developed the courage to use it for my own storytelling as a poet and writer.

Even within her own loquacious family, Mammy was famous for her incessant talking. Her voice was like a radio that was never turned off. It was the soundtrack to my childhood, as constant and inevitable as the rain. Dad was always telling us to keep to ourselves. "Don't be gassing and talking, telling everyone your business. Sure, they'd live in your ear if you let them," he'd say. But Mammy was incorrigibly garrulous and friendly. Dad tried to rein her in, but telling Mammy to stop talking was like trying to stop an avalanche with your bare hands.

Although her formal education was brief—she left school at thirteen to work in Leonards' greengrocer's shop in Dun Laoghaire—she had a marvelous memory and an unerring ear for language. She remembered all the rhymes of her childhood, including the one she and other Catholic children used to sing to tease the Salvation Army followers as they rang their bells along Dun Laoghaire's seafront promenade:

"The Salvation Army, free from sin,
They all went to Heaven in a sardine tin."

There were other rhymes that memorialized the various outbreaks of disease, like the one about whooping cough:

"My mammy told me not to play with you.
Not because you're dirty, not because you're clean.
Because you got the hoopin'-cough
From eatin' margarine."

My childhood memories are inextricably linked with Mammy's quotations from Longfellow, Shakespeare, and Tennyson. Her favorite advice was "To thine own self be true, and it must follow, as the night the day, thou can'st not then be false to any man." She had once played Portia in a school production of "The Merchant of Venice." Thirty years later, she recited speeches with relish. "The quality of mercy is not strained," she'd declaim as she cleaned the hearth on her hands and knees. "It droppeth as the gentle rain from heaven upon the place beneath." She entertained us with droll recitations of "The Owl and the Pussycat" or acted out the tragedy of "The Wreck of the Hesperus." I could just picture the captain lashing his little daughter to the mast, her long skirt billowing out behind her, and the waves crashing over the deck. "If I didn't go to school, I met the scholars coming back," Mammy said proudly. She was an avid reader of adventure stories, which she devoured in bed after we were asleep. Next morning we'd beg her to tell us about the latest chapter of *The Sign of the Spider*, set in deepest darkest Africa, or *The Dog Crusoe*, set in Canada's frozen north.

Mammy seemed to have a bottomless well of proverbs and pithy phrases that she ladled out unexpectedly and with unflagging enthusiasm. "It's many a man's mouth that broke his nose," she'd say, "and what you don't want is dear at a farthing." Her plentiful platitudes were irritating when she used them as spurs to better behavior. "The sun is splitting the stones," she'd announce as she maneuvered around our beds to whisk open the curtains in the morning. "There is a tide in the affairs of men which, taken at the flood, leads on to fortune." All four of us children slept in the same small room for years, fiercely guarding the tiny territory of our individual beds from the others. In the meantime, however, Mammy had us all at her mercy. "Let us then be up and doing!" she'd say as she attempted to pry us out of bed. "When I was your age I used to be up with the lark, riding my bicycle through the Wicklow Mountains, exploring the countryside, instead of sleeping my life away." There was always an implied comparison between us lazy good-for-nothings and she herself, who was up earliest and doing the most. "Ah, don't be always giving out," our Susan would plead from her untidy nest in the corner. But there was no stopping Mammy once she got going. None of us, least of all Dad, could fathom her gift for memorization or her endless aphorisms and household hints. "Leave it to Annie," he would tell us, rolling his eyes. "She'll always have the last word."

The radio with its pink satin face sat in the cupboard beside the fireplace in the living room. It was the center of the household and it taught me early on to love the spoken word. It brought us news, game shows, comedy programs, and advice to the lovelorn in a series of half-hour programs that were sponsored by companies like IMCO Cleaners & Dyers, Jacob's Biscuits, Fry-Cadbury Chocolate, and Glen Abbey, makers of fine nylon stockings. Mammy loved "Woman's Page," a sponsored program hosted by Frankie Byrne. "This is Frankie Byrne with 'Woman's Page,'" the husky voice would commence, "a program for and maybe about you. Now the problems we are discussing today may not be yours, but they could be someday. In any event, 'Woman's Page' draws its material from the lives and events of real people..." I was fascinated by the unhappy housewives who called in to the program and the glimpse of a grown-up world full of romance and heartbreak. Frankie always followed her advice with an upbeat song by Frank Sinatra by way of consolation, or so I assumed.

When she wasn't listening to the radio, Mammy was always singing. One of her favorite songs was "The Blackbird of Sweet Avondale" about the tragic Irish leader, Charles Stuart Parnell. She sang as she washed the breakfast dishes or peeled the potatoes, ballads about young men like Roddy McCorley and Kevin Barry who marched cheerfully to their executions so that "old Ireland might be free." The songs made me almost unbearably sad and I begged her to please stop singing before I burst into tears.

The cupboard under the stairs held Mammy's treasured cookbooks and handwritten recipes, a purple chocolate-box full of family photographs, and an album with lipsticked images of Gary Cooper and Rudolph Valentino from her romantic girlhood. We kept our own bits and bobs in wooden orange crates beside our beds and we wore our cousins' cast-off clothes. We licked our dinner plates and wiped our faces on our sleeves. But Mammy read aloud to us from *Charlotte's Web* and *The Wind in the Willows*, and we thought we were the luckiest family in creation.

In marked contrast to Mammy, Dad was quiet, serious, and suspicious of strangers. He loved rivers and trout fishing. No matter how long he lived in Dublin, he always referred to County Meath as "home." He had *The Meath Chronicle* delivered to the local newsagent's shop, and he devoured every word of it on Saturday afternoons when he sat in his special chair by the fireplace. He often went home at the weekends to shoot and fish with our Uncle John. When he came back on the bus on Sunday night, he laid his brown cardboard suitcase down on a chair and clicked open the locks. There, resting on the sheets of newspaper would be a beautiful pheasant or a fresh speckled trout he had caught that afternoon and wanted Mammy to prepare for dinner.

Dad also went sea fishing off the East Pier in Dun Laoghaire on summer evenings. I loved to trail behind and watch him toss the flatfish with their glassy orange eyes into the rock-pool by the shore. I stared down into the sea's black depths and brooded happily for hours. At home, Mammy tossed the fresh fish in batter and deep-fried them and we feasted night after night on their succulent white flesh.

Dad hated to be cold, and like a cat, he detested getting wet feet, so he would never even put his toe into the freezing waters of the Irish Sea. No matter the season, he always wore a tweed cap for fear of getting his head wet. The cap was a nondescript brown color that had molded itself to the exact shape of his head. Hair-oil had softened the leather band inside to a kid-glove texture. Dad automatically reached for it every time he left the house, set it in place on his head, and adjusted the brim with a practiced gesture. He raised the cap to salute acquaintances on the street. On Sundays, he wore a felt hat out of respect for the Sabbath, but he always donned the cap again on Monday mornings.

Dad loved Irish music and he played the fiddle on Saturday nights in the back rooms of various pubs, although he never touched a drop of alcohol. He didn't have Mammy's gift of the gab, but he was a dab hand at making up stories straight out of his head. We all loved his story about Sunny, the black doll. I passionately wanted a black doll, although the only non-white people I'd ever seen in the flesh were one or two Indian medical students in Dublin and a Chinese doctor at Saint Michael's Hospital in Dun Laoghaire. For that matter, the only non-Catholics I'd ever seen were the Protestant girls from Clarinda

Park School in Glasthule when they marched in a long line down to the seafront for their chaperoned weekend walks. They wore matching dark blue uniforms with funny-looking flat hats on their heads. They were fairly exotic, but I thought black people must be even more so, and I insisted that I wanted a black doll. Dad promised to bring one back from one of his trips to visit his sisters in Somerset. When he came home with the doll in hand, he told us all about his trip.

"You see, the trouble was that Sunny had never been in a plane before," he said, handing over my new toy. "And she wanted to try everything." We had never been in a plane either, only to the airport, so we could easily relate to Sunny's feelings. "It was a twin-engine Dakota airplane," he went on. "I sat her down beside me in her own seat and fastened her in with the seat-belt. She loved the sugar-cubes the air-hostess brought for her, all individually wrapped in paper. They were just the right size for a doll." Dad always brought sugar-cubes home for us from his various trips to England so we nodded gravely at this detail. "Everything would have been fine except that Sunny kept slipping out of her seat belt to go exploring. She has a naturally curious disposition," Dad said. I held Sunny out in front of me. She did seem to have a mischievous glint in her black eyes; a drop of divilment was what Dad called it. "One time she disappeared and I couldn't find her anywhere," he continued. He and the air-hostess searched all over the plane and finally discovered Sunny down in the baggage compartment. "I was never so relieved in my life," he said.

Dad's story gave Sunny so much life that she took on a personality that the other dolls, Eileen, Roisín, and Belinda, never achieved. A few years later when Sunny's eyes fell into the back of her head, Dad came to the rescue. He took her out to his shed, pried off the top of her head, and replaced the rubber band that held her eyes in place. "Now, *Alanna*," he said, handing me the doll. "You'd do well to keep her very quiet for a few days. She's just undergone eye surgery." I was terribly impressed and followed his instructions to the letter.

High Tea at a Low Table

Chapter Three

Although she always seemed youthful, Mammy was at least ten years older than were the mothers of other children our age. She had almost given up on marriage when she met Dad, and she was thirty-five when they finally got around to tying the knot. In addition to looking after John and me, at ages four and two respectively, she gave birth to the twins when she was forty-two. It must have been a terrible blow when her own mother died while she was pregnant with the twins. All of these factors had a huge impact on her health, although it was all a mystery to us at the time. The twins were still only infants when Mammy was diagnosed with rheumatic fever and sent to Loughlinstown Hospital, an awe-inspiring edifice that had been built on the site of the local workhouse.

Dad brought us to visit Mammy on Sunday afternoons. We took the single-decker 45A bus from the Bray Road to what was, in those days, the country. Children were not allowed into the hospital so we had to content ourselves with standing on tiptoe on a grassy hillock outside and being lifted up occasionally to look at her through the barred windows of the ward. Those were miserable visits. Once, Dad's friend Jerry Meagher smuggled me into the ward under his overcoat, but we were spotted by the matron and cast out again before I could run to Mammy's arms. Still, we consoled ourselves, we were all at home, and we knew where Mammy was. After a time the situation became more difficult. There was no one to look after us when Dad was at work, so it was decided that we three girls should be sent to Saint Joseph's Orphanage in Tivoli Road, Dun Laoghaire, to be cared for by The Daughters of the Heart of Mary. Saint Joseph's was a girls-only institution, so other plans had to be made for John. He was to be sent to live with our relations in County Meath.

One day Dad took me down to the Orphanage on the big green double-decker bus. We got off at Tivoli Road and walked up to the imposing front door of the convent. Dad pressed the bell and the door was opened by a woman with grey hair done up in a bun. She wore a grey knee-length skirt and jacket. She ushered us inside in hushed tones and pointed to the doorway on the left. I could see it was a kind of chapel with women kneeling at long benches. I caught a glimpse of a glowing red light through the doorway. Another woman emerged from a door at the end of the hall. She was dressed like the first one except that she had brown hair and wore a brown skirt and jacket instead of a grey one. She greeted Dad deferentially and asked us to follow her out through another door into a garden. The woman took my left hand and I held on tightly to Dad's hand with my right. The two of them talked over my head as we made our way slowly up a long path with flowers on each side.

The scent of the flowers was like perfume. It made me sleepy. Suddenly I realized that Dad's hand was gone and the woman was holding my left hand more tightly than before. I turned around and saw Dad's back vanishing down the lane. In an instant, I realized what was happening—I was being abandoned. I wrenched myself away from the woman and ran screaming after Dad. He picked me up and I clung to him with all my strength. The woman came bustling towards us. "Oh now, now," she said, "such carry-on. She'll be grand, Mr. Goggins. Don't worry." Dad looked stricken but he shook his head. "I can't do it, Sister," he said. I held on to him, gulping huge sobs, all the way home to Sallynoggin.

Chapter Four

After the orphanage episode there was not much choice but to send me off to the country with John. We lived with various aunts, uncles, and cousins in County Meath. I remember waking up one night in Uncle John and Aunt Ita's living room in Trim after sleepwalking down the stairs in my long nightdress. We also stayed with Aunt Julia, who had four or five children, and with Aunt May and Uncle Willie, who had about seven children at the time. There was Liam and Dessie and Sheila and Seany and Seamus and I couldn't remember the rest. Aunt Ita was tall and thin with a kind face and clever hands. She had no little girls of her own, so she sewed pretty polka-dot dresses with matching knickers for me. When the aunts and uncles spoke, they sounded like Dad. Their words seemed to rush together and run uphill and down again suddenly, as if they were riding on a pony and trap. They called Dad Jimmy, while everyone else, including Mammy, called him Jim.

Dad came down on the bus to County Meath to see us every other weekend. I always cried and begged him to take me home when we saw him off at the bus stop in Trim. I held on to the bus stop pole so tightly that the kind relations had to pry my fingers off to get me to leave. It was only later that I realized what a lonely life it must have been for Dad, visiting us in the country one weekend, the twins at the orphanage on the weekends in-between, and Mammy in hospital on weeknights after work. She did her best to encourage him with letters from the hospital. In one, dated March 1956, entitled "St. Brigid's Ward, Tuesday morning," she wrote:

"Dear Jim,
I am feeling quite upset this morning as I have been moved out of

my nice little room up to where my poor mother was. I had hoped my next move would be home but some other person has come in who needs to be very quiet and, of course, I am well enough to be moved now. I got the Sister to phone up about the twins this morning. The reply was "Nothing to worry about, doing very nicely." You have to believe them and hope for the best, the poor little pets. …..I have allowed the children to take up so much of my time lately, and I've been so tired that I'm quite out of the way of telling you how much I love you. But I do love you, dear, just as much as when we were first married. I used to put all the nice things in my mind off to some distant future when I'd have lots of time. But that might never come and why not make the most of the present which is ours? Thank you, darling, for making me so happy. Perhaps this separation will have been good for both of us. I'll have to close now, dearest, and send you all my love until we meet again.

Your Loving Wife, Annie XX."

Eventually Mammy recovered and John and I were reunited with her and Dad. But she had to visit the orphanage several times before she could persuade the twins to come home with her. They were only infants when they went in, she explained, and the nuns had weaned and toilet-trained them in the meantime. They had been there at least a year and they didn't know Mammy anymore.

I wondered why we didn't just leave them where they were. After all, what could Mammy and Dad possibly want with twins when they had me? Nevertheless, one Sunday afternoon we went to the orphanage to get the twins and we all rode the bus home to Sallynoggin. The twins were quaintly dressed in pinafores with white handkerchiefs pinned to their collars. They had huge dolls with plastic faces in their arms. Once we got home, they wouldn't let Mammy out of their sight. Mary followed Mammy around all day asking, "Am I a good girl, Mammy?" over and over again and Mammy always told her that she was. Mammy said that Mary had always taken to her while Susan had always taken to Dad ever since they were born. After the orphanage, they clung to their favorite parent more than ever. Susan had terrible nightmares and she always woke up calling for Dad. He had had nightmares himself as a child, and he never failed to get up and come into our room to comfort her.

Mammy and Dad often talked about what a terrible time it was when we were all separated and how grateful they were to be together again. They never tried to hide what happened, although there must have been plenty of heartbreak we didn't understand. But they never seemed to mind retelling the stories. One of our favorites was about the time the twins caught whooping cough. It was early on in their stay at the Orphanage and they were sent to Cherry Orchard Fever Hospital in Clonskea, County Dublin. Visiting hours were strictly enforced, and Dad couldn't always get there in time after his work. There was a lovely nurse who had black hair and a kind smile, Dad said, and she would let him into the hospital at non-visiting hours to look at the twins who were quarantined behind the glass door of the ward. Afterwards she would give him a cup of tea in the hospital kitchen. But the problem was the red-haired nurse, who was big and buxom and a real stickler for the rules. We were told that, like all red-haired people, she had a terrible temper. When she was on duty, Dad was ushered out as soon as visiting hour was over.

The Red-haired Nurse and the Black-haired Nurse became our symbols of good and evil. "Daddy, Daddy, tell us the story about the Black-haired Nurse and the Red-haired Nurse," we asked him over and over again and he always obliged. I loved imagining him there in the hospital, drinking his tea like a character in a book in which everything turned out well and we all lived happily ever after.

Chapter Five

Mammy's original home at Number 19 Findlater Street was a tiny pre-World War I row house with an outside toilet and no bathroom. A talking parrot named "Polly," a gift from a relation who had sailed to foreign parts, lived for years in a cage inside the front door. Sometimes Granny got tired of his constant chat. "Would someone ever throw a blanket over that oul' bird," she'd say. "He has me demented with his talking." There were other relatives who did not return from foreign parts. Mammy's Uncle Edward Swords was killed by a shell in Weehawee, China, at the outbreak of the First World War in 1914. Mammy and her sister Kathleen used to play with his war medals when they were children. Unfortunately, family rumor had it, their brother Pat pawned them later on for the price of a pint.

Some of Granny Swords' sisters had worked as servants in the "Big Houses" of the so-called Anglo-Irish Ascendancy. Her sister Mary served as a cook and housekeeper for Miss Moses of Leeson Street, Dublin. Another sister, Annie, worked as a housekeeper at Cawbawn Lane, Shanganagh, where a gruesome murder had taken place sometime during the 1920s. A package of yellowed newspapers in the cupboard under the stairs at our house was produced as evidence of the incident, including a description of a bloody hatchet that was found near the scene of the crime. It was wonderfully chilling to think that dark and violent acts had come so close to our inconsequential lives. Little could I imagine that, later on in America, the violent act of being kidnapped would intrude on my life and the lives of those I loved.

The New World seemed impossibly far away in those days. Mammy said that Bride Kane, one of Granny's cousins from Ballygannon, County Wicklow, had gone to Canada on a visit as a young woman, but she was so seasick on the way over that she stayed for forty years. When she finally returned, her vocabulary was full of strange new words that embarrassed her relatives. "It's on the bureau, Ellen," she'd announce. "What on earth is a *bureau*?" Granny would mutter in exasperation. "Wouldn't you think Bridie would have learned how to speak properly in America?"

Some of my favorite stories about Mammy's early life concerned the Black and Tans, the special force sent to Ireland by the British in the early 1920s to quell the Irish rebels and intimidate the people. Their name came from the clothing they wore, consisting of a combination of dark green Royal Irish Constabulary police uniforms and army khakis. The Tans used to knock at Granny's door with their rifle-butts as they made their way up Findlater Street. When she heard the knock, Granny made the children kneel down on the kitchen floor to pray. "There's only women and children here," she'd call out through the keyhole and then they'd wait, holding their breaths, until the sound of marching feet had died away. My grandfather, Patrick Swords, worked for the Irish Lights, a company that manned the lighthouses around the coast of Ireland. Because he worked for an English company, the family was relatively safe from harassment by the Tans. The Smiths, who lived across the street, had sons in the IRA and they were regularly woken up and dragged out in the middle of the night.

Granny worried about her own sons during The Troubles and often went out looking for them when they were late coming home. One night she was walking home along the "Metals," as the path next to the railway line was called, when she noticed an unnaturally large black dog with fiery eyes that was keeping pace with her. She was convinced it was some manifestation of the devil and she prayed fervently all the way home. Just as she neared her own street, the dog mysteriously disappeared. This kind of story sent delicious shivers up and down my spine and renewed my belief in the power of evil, if not in the power of good.

After she got married and her mother died, Mammy's only sister

Kathleen lived at Number 19 with Aunt May, Uncle Pat and our cousin Martin. My brother and sisters and I adored Aunt Kathleen and we liked Uncle Pat and Aunt May who were always genial and didn't seem to mind our frequent visits. Long, rectangular pictures of Edwardian ladies hung on the livingroom walls. There was a tiny scullery with a black gas cooker. The outside toilet smelled of whitewash and had a high, wooden toilet seat and a long chain with a wooden handle. In Mammy's day people used to go to the public bathhouse down by the seafront, known to one and all as simply The Baths. Seaweed baths were particularly popular because they were supposed to be good for rheumatism, but you could soak in all manner of marine concoctions, from hot seawater to sulphur, alkaline and Russian baths, depending on your particular ailment.

Given the lack of washing facilities at Findlater Street, Mammy had great reverence for baths in Sallynoggin. You had to have a good fire going for several hours in the boiler-grate before there was enough hot water to fill the bathtub, so Mammy usually took a bath long after we were in bed. She loved scented soap and always placed a big box of talcum powder with a feathery powder-puff next to the tub. There were ladies' magazines and novels, hand-lotion and clouds of steam when we barged in late at night to go to the toilet in the middle of her ablutions.

Physically speaking, Mammy was short and generously proportioned. "It's better to say *there you are* than *where are you*," she said in defense of her buxom figure. She loved the sea and was a great swimmer. In the summer, she took us down to the seafront at Dun Laoghaire where she had gone swimming as a child. We called it Bugrock, although she said the real name was Scotsman's Bay. Her strong arms took her far out into the waves until she was barely a speck on our horizon and we cried for her to swim back to us. Sometimes we met Miss Smith, the spinster nurse who had been a customer in Leonards' greengrocers' shop where Mammy had worked before she got married. Miss Smith was terribly old and bony. She had thin white hair pinned up in a bun and she wore a long, baggy, black wool swimsuit. She swam every day in a straight line out to sea and back again. Mammy said she was a very refined Protestant lady. We understood from Mammy's tone of voice that Miss Smith might swim in our sea, but she lived in a separate realm to which there was no admittance for the likes of us.

I never thought of Mammy as an old woman, although she was seventy-four by the time she died in 1988. There was always an air of playfulness about her. In my mind's eye, she appears in a series of family photos that caught her in the prime of her forties and fifties. In one such image, she is standing in the backyard of our house in Pearse Close, clutching her bicycle by the handlebars. She has just come in from shopping, and the basket on the front of the bike is full of groceries, or *messages*, as we referred to them. She is wearing a dark coat and a beret. She looks robust, smiling at our John who is taking the picture with her old Brownie camera. It's lunchtime and, if she hurries, she'll be able to catch today's episode of "The Kennedys of Castleross" on the radio. Days when she misses the program because some woman kept her talking - *moryah* - John listens to "The Kennedys" and recounts the entire episode, describing Mrs. Kennedy's trials and the postmistress's gossip—the storms in the teacup of Irish country life.

Mammy was a woman of unquestionably good intentions. "God help that poor unfortunate," she would exclaim, making the sign of the cross, whenever she heard the scream of an ambulance or saw a handicapped person. She knitted string vests for us from white cotton yarn. They ended up as floor cloths after they were worn out or had stretched so much that they reached to our ankles. She started an *Aran* jumper for our John's First Communion when he was six and she hadn't finished by the time of his Confirmation when he was ten and far too big for it. But she was a good cook who specialized in soda bread and sweetcakes. "I know what we'll do," she'd say if the weather was gloomy. "We'll have high tea at a low table just to be posh." Then she'd produce one of her special sponge-cakes with homemade jam in the middle and a flurry of icing-sugar on top. Dad loved her apple pie and lemon curd. We traded lumps of her homemade toffee with other children at school, and we moithered her into making her ginger biscuits for tea and her paper-thin pancakes for Shrove Tuesday.

Mammy had a very expressive face and a lovely voice for telling stories. Her tales of narrow escapes from rising sea tides and near drownings had us all on the edges of our seats. Her stories often described the changes that had taken place in Ireland since she was a girl. She told us about the "glimmer man" who inspected gas-stoves during the war to make sure people were not using the rationed gas. A child was posted on the corner as a lookout while the gas was in use, and housewives kept wet cloths at the ready to cool the burners. I loved her story about Aunt Kathleen's friend from Woolworth's who emigrated with her daughter to the state of Louisiana. Mammy, who had never been out of Ireland but who loved adventure stories, described the alligator-ridden swamps of Louisiana and the low-hanging trees where a snake might drop down on top of you when you least expected it. She said the daughter was a beautiful child with liquid brown eyes and long, abundant, dark hair. Unfortunately, all her strength must have gone into her hair, for she fell into a decline and was never the same again.

Mammy was a devout Catholic and her imagination was rich in symbolism. Saints and angels peopled her interior universe—an old man carrying the Christ-child on his shoulders; a black cross burned into a donkey's back to honor the place where Jesus sat during his entry into Jerusalem; birds gathered around the tonsured head of St. Francis of Assisi. From time to time, Mammy attended religious weekend retreats at Saint Joseph's convent on Tivoli Road in Dun Laoghaire. Dad loved to tease her about the impossibility of her remaining silent for an entire weekend. He enjoyed fantasies of a quiet life, preferably in a Trappist monastery where the monks took a vow of silence. Or perhaps he remembered the story of Mammy's three male cousins who came from Kilcoole, County Wicklow. Some ancient feud had occurred between them whose origins were long forgotten. They lived together in the same house until they were old men without resolving their differences and died in the end without ever speaking to each other.

Those country cousins were the exception in an otherwise affable family. Mammy's first cousin Richard Coleman charmed us all when he came home from New York in 1960. He and his wife Maisie seemed like beings from another planet with their tanned skin and American accents and Maisie's blue-rinsed hair. They lived with us in the little four-room house in Sallynoggin for three months when I was eight years old. One of our Mary's images from that time is of watching Aunt Maisie rinse her knickers out in the white porcelain kitchen sink. I cannot imagine where everyone slept or how the four adults managed to get along in such close proximity.

But for the four of us children it was three months of bliss and fascination. Uncle Dick and Aunt Maisie brought me a Davy Crockett buckskin jacket that I wore until I was twelve and could no longer even pretend it fit me. Uncle Dick captured my heart by playing "Home On The Range" on his mandolin. Their visit was the occasion for a major *hooley* at the Workmen's Club in Dun Laoghaire. All our cousins, aunts and uncles, and Dad's musical friends were there. Everyone danced and the children skated over the chalky dance-floor in their stockinged feet.

Thus began my long romance with America. Like all romances, it was fraught with unforeseen difficulty. But I can still recapture that first feeling of infatuation with everything that was alien and therefore, to me, exotic and desirable.

Chapter Six

There was nothing exotic or desirable about the man with the gun. I could see he was nervous from the way he kept running his hand through his dark hair every few minutes. He looked to be about my own age but it was hard to tell from his unkempt appearance. "Don't do anything stupid and you'll be okay," the man said. "And stop shaking!" When he spoke, it was the gun I heard talking.

Once we were out on the interstate, he seemed to relax, although he reminded me from time to time that he would kill me if we were pulled over for speeding. "This is a terrible car," he said accusingly, as if it was my fault he had picked a lemon. Near Waterbury, I noticed a sign that read "$500 fine for carrying firearms." I glanced over at the gun in his lap and he picked it up and pointed it at me. Then he set it down and took a pack of cigarettes out of his shirt pocket, lit one, and offered the pack to me. I'd been trying to quit but this didn't seem like the time to quibble. I took a cigarette and lit up.

It dawned on me that I wasn't due to pick up my son for several days, so it would be a long time before anyone missed me. I was terrified, sitting there trapped in my own car as it rattled down the highway. But on another level, I was not surprised. My everyday life in America as a single mother newly separated from husband and homeland was so terrifying that being kidnapped at gunpoint seemed like just another unfortunate occurrence. I thought about recent mornings and waking up in my apartment by the Winooski River, feeling heavy, leaden, oppressed. Trying to tear myself loose from my dreams, their wispy tendrils still clinging to me as I swam up toward the light. I kept trying to dig down to whatever was below the gloom but it felt as if I was trying to lift a manhole-cover. Was there really energy and anger down there at some lower geologic level? But no, the familiar internal voice kicked in with its ceaseless diatribe. There's something wrong with you, some congenital deficiency. You're no fun. Always complaining, always unhappy. You're never satisfied, that's your problem. That's what got you into this mess. You're here all alone in America, where it's nobody's job to look after you. Why should anyone care about you? You've made a hames of it now alright, you dullamoo, and all because you would not be said or led by anyone.

"Talk," the man said, "talk to me." And so I did, babbling about my job with handicapped kids and then about how I was a single mother with no money, putting myself through school. I knew I was laying it on a bit thick but it wasn't all that far from the truth. "Jesus," the man muttered. "Out of everyone I could have chosen, why did I have to pick you?"

Chapter Seven

Coming from the country as he did, Jim Goggins, my Dad, was the outsider in our family and on our street. His muscled thinness contrasted keenly with Mammy's soft, warm contours. He spoke with a country accent and he used many strange words that turned out to be Irish. He called a jumper a *gansey* and a corner-boy a *bowsey*. I was his *Alanna* and our John was his *Amhic* or *Gossún*. Instead of a simple "no," he said "divil a bit," and he told Mammy to "whisht" when he wanted to get a word in edgeways. "Be the hokey farmer," he'd say to her, putting down his newspaper. "This fella here knows as much about our problems as a dog knows about his father. Sure he wouldn't know B from a bull's foot!" This way of talking marked Dad as a foreigner and his shyness made him awkward in company.

Nevertheless, our lives revolved around Dad. He was the lynchpin of our universe and he was the source of the problem, the force, the wedge, the spanner in the works. Most important of all, he was the breadwinner on whom we all depended.

Whenever I displayed a tendency towards gloom, my country ancestry was invoked by the Dublin relatives. "She's a real Goggins," they would say, scrutinizing my dark hair and sullen expression, nodding their heads in agreement. I knew such a pronouncement was not intended as a compliment and that there was no escape from the prison of their opinions. I was the spitting image of Dad and I had obviously inherited his moody-broody disposition as well. I wished with all my heart that I had been born a boy like John. He was good-tempered, intelligent, and in all ways admirable, as far as I was concerned. I felt like a poor excuse for a girl with my jealous nature and romantic notions, not to mention my hair, which Dad cut short and sheared up the back of my neck with his metal clippers.

Long before we heard about Dad's missing eye, we knew that his early life had been harsh and much more difficult than Mammy's magical childhood days in Dublin. That was why he didn't talk about his childhood as much as Mammy did about hers. When he described life in the country, his stories always had a bitter edge to them. He was the fourth of seven children, a bashful child who had hated to be teased for his bashfulness. His principal torturer was his Aunt Jane, whom he referred to as "a contrary oul' faggot." Dad promised that he would never let anyone treat us the way he had been treated. His father had had a habit of making promises he didn't fulfill—to take young Jimmy fishing, to buy him a fishing rod, to take him to the races. Jimmy would wait and wait but the promised treat never materialized. Dad said he would never make a promise to a child and then let him down, and we believed him. Such a vow was part of his sternness and pride in his good name.

Before she was married, Dad's mother had worked "in service" at one of the Big Houses for twelve shillings a year. Julia, the eldest of her seven children, was born in 1912, followed by Susan fourteen months later, then May in 1916, Dad in 1918, then John, William, and finally Ann in 1928. His mother cooked all the meals over the open fireplace. She kept hens, and Dad had an uncle who used to juggle the eggs for entertainment. Dad did not come from farming people. Grandad worked on the railway branch line that ran from Kilmessan to Athboy. He was known as "a miles man" because he had to walk the line every day, inspecting the railway ties (or sleepers as they were called) to make sure they hadn't rotted from waterlogging. The rails were kept in place with wooden keys that expanded and contracted with the weather. According to John, who was always a lover of trains and railways, Grandad would have carried a big long-handled wrench and a long hammer for knocking the various parts back into place. When he lost his job in 1931, the family fell on hard times. However, Grandad was never a man to seek his fortune abroad. *Coras Iompair Eireann*, or C.I.E., the Irish transportation company, offered him a transfer to Bray, County Wicklow, about forty miles away. But Grandad had no desire to leave home and he turned the offer down. Instead, he got a temporary job as a manual laborer with the County Council, and the family had to struggle along as best it could.

Dad's Uncle Jack Goggins left for America at the age of twenty-three or twenty-four after a few years in the Irish Army, Cavalry division. He became a corrections officer at Sing-Sing prison and returned home for a visit in 1933, the only one of the five who ever came back to Ireland. Dad's uncle Pat was a guitar-player who traveled around the United States. He ended up an alcoholic in New York City. "It must have been an extraordinary change," Dad said philosophically, "to come from the wilds of County Meath and to be imprisoned in the box that was New York." Years later when I found myself homesick for Dublin in the wilds of Vermont, those words came back to haunt me in reverse.

Dad's family was poor enough but there were others that were poorer still. One day when Dad was five years old, he was outside in the yard, helping his mother to churn butter. An old man came down the road and leaned over the front gate. He wore a long brown coat and a soft hat that shaded his eyes. "God bless all here," he said, touching his hat to Granny. "I've been walking the roads all day, Missus, and I'm nearly famished with the hunger. I wonder would you have a sup of buttermilk to spare?" "Sit down there now," she said, wiping her hands on her apron and indicating a wooden bench set against the whitewashed wall. "I'll go and get it for you." She went into the house and came back with a big mug of buttermilk. The man was very thankful. "God bless you, Missus," he said, "and may the giving hand never falter." He drank the milk in one long gulp, smacking his lips and then wiping them with a big handkerchief that he took out of the back pocket of his trousers.

"I'm on me way to the Workhouse over in Trim," the man told them. "Sure I can't manage any longer on me own." He knew the right direction but he wasn't sure which turn to take at the crossroads above the house. (In those days, every field in County Meath had a name. There was "The Crackeen," "The Church Field," "The River Meadow," "The Toher Field," and "The Well Field.") "Go on up that way," said Granny, pointing towards a break in the long line of overgrown hedgerows that bordered both sides of the road, "then turn right at the stile by the Toher Field." The man thanked her and walked out towards the road. For some reason, Dad was terribly worried that the man would lose his way. He ran after him and tugged at the man's tattered coat. Then he grabbed a big handful of green grass and threw it down on the road. With his finger, he drew a map of the way ahead. "You see here, Mister," he said, drawing a line in the grass. "Don't take that road, take this one." To his immense surprise, the man put his hand in his pocket, drew out a copper penny and gave it to him. "It was my first penny and it was a great big black one," Dad said. "Sure I thought I was rich!"

Apart from the poverty, class distinction was also rife in the country. There was a vast social distance between the ordinary working poor and those who were well off enough to live in the big houses and educate their children at private schools. By way of illustration, Dad told us about a poor elderly couple, Patsy and Mary Connell, who lived down the road in Addinstown, half way between the two towns of Trim and Athboy. In those days, there was no gas or electricity, no running water or shops between the two towns, a distance of seven miles. One day Patsy had the misfortune to break his ankle and the doctor had to be called. Mary decided she had better wash the ankle before the doctor's visit. She hobbled up the road to get a bucket of water from the pump, boiled it in a pot over the fire, and with great difficulty, scrubbed the injured ankle clean. "Dr. Connie O'Reilly was a contrary oul' divil with no time for the poor," Dad told us. "He knocked on the door and Mary led him into the bedroom. When he pulled back the sheet that covered Patsy, he saw one black foot and one white foot. 'Isn't it a pity now,' he sneered in his grand Anglo-Irish accent, 'that he didn't break the both of them?'"

Another neighbor by the name of Paddy Kennedy lived alone near Dad's house. Paddy used to amble along the road smoking his pipe in the heel of the evening. One day Dad and the other lads were playing football in the road. One of them kicked the ball and it hit Paddy Kennedy right in the gob, knocking the pipe out of his mouth. The tobacco spilled out on to the road. The lads, who were terrified of Paddy anyway, ran as fast as they could in the opposite direction. Paddy shook his fist at their retreating backs. "Oh, there's no doubt," he shouted, "the breedin' is more important than the feedin'. And furthermore," he added for good measure, "the mothers that raised you would drown nothing!"

When my parents were young, the Church still ruled the hearts and minds of the people. Dad told us about the parish priest in Athboy who was fond of poking the bushes alongside the road with his blackthorn stick to roust out courting couples. At Sunday mass, he read out the names of parishioners who had failed to contribute to the support of their pastors and verbally abused them in front of the congregation. "He would sweat blood if he saw a woman in a sleeveless dress," Dad said.

To offset the authoritarian stranglehold of the Church, people told stories that made fun of its rituals and undermined its influence. The altar boys in our neighborhood did not have much understanding of Latin, despite the best efforts of the Christian Brothers, whose motto was, "Boys who can learn and won't learn must be made learn." Altar boys were famous for making up phrases that sounded like Latin to insert into the liturgy. When they recited the solemn *Confiteor* during Mass, they would substitute for "*Mea culpa, mea culpa, mea maxima culpa*" the words "Me a cowboy, me a cowboy, me a Mexican cowboy." And "*A deum que laetificat, juven tutem maem*" translated into "Adam stole the pussycat, the Jewman got the blame."

Uncle Willie, Dad's younger brother, was a big, red-faced man who didn't drink or smoke but he ate sweets by the pound. He always had a paper bag full of Bulls' Eyes and Jelly-Babies in his pocket. He had a musical Meath accent that was stronger than Dad's and a good-humored laugh. One day he drove up from the country to bring us a few stones of coal and a dozen fresh eggs. While he was having his tea, Uncle Willie told Dad a story about a fellow who was "a bit fond of the drink." At the time in question, the Mission was underway in Athboy parish church. Every parish had an annual mission led by pairs of visiting Jesuit or Redemptorist priests. It was a kind of spiritual spring-cleaning. The first week was for the women, since they were responsible for the spiritual as well as the physical welfare of their families. The second week was devoted to the men, and the third week to the children. Nightly Sodality meetings were held at the church and the week ended with Confession on Saturday, followed by Holy Communion on Sunday morning. The Mission had a "revival tent" atmosphere, although that term had not yet been introduced to the Irish psyche.

On the last night of the men's mission in Athboy, the whole group was supposed to publicly renounce its sins. The priest surveyed the passive congregation of men in their dark clothes and bare heads, most of whom had been bullied into attending by their good-living, God-fearing wives. He called out in a loud voice: "Do you renounce Satan and all his works and pomps?" A low mumble arose from the men. "Louder," the priest shouted, "I can't hear you." Still not much response. "Louder again," says the priest. "Do you renounce the Devil and all his works and pomps?" Uncle Willie's friend roused himself from a drunken stupor. "Ah, feck him," he shouted into the suddenly deafening silence. "That put the cap and cloak on it," Uncle Willie said with some satisfaction.

When we complained about school, Dad told us about the one he had attended as a child. "Kilbride National School was built in 1847 and it was a wreck," he said, "with neither water nor electricity nor gas nor feck-all. It smelled like bodies and toilets. The teacher was from Kildermot and she bet everything into us, including religion. We had to walk two-and-a-half to three miles to school and most of the time we didn't have shoes. My mother used to make shirts for us out of eight-stone flour bags. The hard part was getting the stain of the writing out of the bags."

In 1932 at the age of fourteen, Dad left Kilbride School. He was glad to get a secondhand bicycle to ride in to the Technical School in Trim. "I loved it there," he said. "It was the last word in terrazzo floors and all sorts of things. I used to do odd jobs for farmers or anyone I could work for during the summer holidays to pay for schoolbooks. I worked for eight shillings a week making hay during the summers of 1932, '33, and '34. The hay used to be put up in cocks and then headed so it looked like a thatched house." Dad's ambition was to become an agricultural inspector, but in September 1933, the accident in which he lost his eye put paid to his hopes and dreams. He left school and moved to Dublin where he tried his hand at milking cows for a while. Later he got a job at a nursery garden called Birchgrove. The Walker family lived in the Big House where Dad's sister May worked as a servant. He was given a room in an outhouse and was told to address the Walker children as "Master Gerald," "Master John," and "Miss Joan." May eventually returned home to County Meath to get married but Dad stayed on at Birchgrove for a total of eleven years. He bicycled back and forth to County Meath most weekends, a distance of over thirty miles each way.

While he was at Birchgrove, Dad recalled that new houses were being built nearby at Monkstown Farm. "The workers spent fifty hours a week up to their knees in muck," he told us disgustedly as we passed that area on our Sunday walks. "They were mixing concrete to build the walls. Concrete blocks hadn't been invented yet. They earned thirty-two shillings and sixpence a week. Eventually they went on strike for more money. All of them had wives and children, but it was six full winter months before they came back to work. And all they got," he continued, shaking his finger at us, "was an extra two shillings and sixpence a week for their trouble!" I knew that as a van-driver, Dad belonged to the Irish Transport and General Workers

Union, which was founded by the great labor leader, Jim Larkin. Dad was proud of his union membership and he freely quoted from the Scriptures in support of the working man. "The poor we have always with us," he would intone bitterly, especially when he came home from work, tired and soaked to the skin after riding his bike in the rain. "The laborer is worthy of his hire." But although he paid lip-service to Socialism, Dad was not the kind of man to step out of line against the Church and the status quo. A man like him, with a wife and four children to support, had little economic or political power. All the more reason why he ruled the tiny kingdom of his family, his house, and his garden like a not-so-benevolent despot.

After many years at Birchgrove, Dad moved into "digs" at White's Terrace, Donnybrook, under the sway of an infamous landlady by the name of Lizzie Green. "If you didn't eat your boiled egg at breakfast time, she'd serve the same egg up to you again for dinner," Dad said. "I was et alive with fleas and mice and half-starved into the bargain." When he left the digs at six in the morning to cycle to work, Lizzie would shake holy water on him in lieu of giving him a proper breakfast. "God bless you now, Jimmy," she'd call out, "sure you'll be grand!" Things improved when Dad's sister Sue came to Dublin to work as a nurse. She lived on Brighton Road. "I often got sick riding the five and a half miles from Donnybrook to Birchgrove," Dad said. "I used to visit my sister to get a decent meal. This was in the early '40s. She'd give me a bag of apples that would keep me going for the week. Except for that, I would have been famished with the hunger."

Eventually Dad moved out to Sallynoggin in south County Dublin to live with Tom Byrne in Number 4 Longford Villas. Tom's brother, Jack the Milkman, lived next door in Number 5. "Tom's other brother Ned was a terrible little weasel," Dad said. "He had been gassed in the First World War and he brought home a piece of lead the size of a half-crown that had been taken out of his leg. He used to box the wall when he had been drinking. Of course Tom Byrne himself was a divil for drinking vinegar," Dad went on reflectively. "He bought it by the gallon and he used to lash it on to his dinner. I don't know if it ever did him any good."

In the evenings Tom Byrne taught Dad to play the fiddle, a skill he cherished all his life. He bought his first fiddle from Pat Mellon, who had a second-hand shop on Patrick Street, Dun Laoghaire. "He was a Wexford man and a decent man," Dad said decisively. The fiddle cost seven shillings and sixpence, a considerable sum for a man earning only ten shillings a week.

Tom Byrne was a manager at Leonards' greengrocers shop in Dun Laoghaire where Mammy worked. It was he who introduced Dad to Mammy. Dad drove the van that delivered produce to Leonards' from Birchgrove Nursery. Mammy and Dad got acquainted over the vegetables, she upbraiding him for their poor quality; he country-shy, only a messenger-boy, marveling at her gift for putting him profoundly in his place. Dad described her as "very bright and absolutely honest. She wouldn't say a bad word about anyone although she had a lot to put up with as a shop assistant." He added, "If oulwans only wanted a pound of sausages, they'd send a van to deliver them to the house." Dad's first date with her was to Murdochs' staff dance at Ross's Hotel in Dun Laoghaire in December 1942. One of the Leonards' boys was given two tickets to the dance and he passed them on to Mammy. Forty years later, Dad still vividly remembered the royal blue, satin dress she wore to that dance. She had rescued him from a life of loneliness and he was always grateful.

My parents were married in 1948 in Mammy's parish church of Glasthule. He was thirty years old and she was thirty-five. Granny did not trust country people like Dad, so it had been a long engagement. He brought Mammy home one night, ten minutes after their 11:00 o'clock curfew. Granny opened the door to their knock. "Annie," she said, grabbing her daughter's arm and pulling her inside. "It's ten past eleven. You're not wed yet, you know." For their honeymoon, Mammy and Dad put their bicycles on the train and spent their holiday cycling around County Wicklow. Always, for me, the names of Woodenbridge, Arklow, and Roundwood—all the places they visited—were tinged with romance. I liked to picture them, poor but still young and carefree, cycling through The Garden of Ireland where it was always sunny and leafy green.

After their honeymoon, they moved to 21 Crosthwaite Park in Dun Laoghaire where their first child, John, was born in 1950. Later they moved to Corrig Avenue to act as caretakers for Mr. Percy Packenham's Bridge Club. I was born during this sojourn in 1952.

Dad was always a gardener by instinct and inclination. He grew loganberries in Corrig Avenue and, when we moved to Sallynoggin, brought five or six of the plants to transfer to the garden there. He was one of the few people in the neighborhood to take pride in his house and garden, despite the fact that he had no hope of ever owning the place until we were long grown and out of the house for good.

Chapter Eight

The Bridge Club was Georgian in style with three storeys and a basement. In exchange for their caretaking, my parents had a rent-free flat in the basement and the use of a garden in the back that Dad planted with fruit bushes, vegetables and flowers. All the relations on both sides of my family had been servants in the Big Houses of the Anglo-Irish aristocracy and caretaking was not much of a step up from there. Still it was a happy time for everyone. Granny Swords was still alive and Mammy was very attached to her. Granny was never one to keep her opinions to herself and, according to Dad, she always answered every question that was asked, whether or not it was addressed to her. It was she who decided I would be called Angela because I was born at twelve o'clock when the *Angelus* bells were ringing. Two years earlier, just before our John was born, when everyone was wondering would it be a boy or a girl, Granny had to put her oar in. "What matter whether 'tis a boy or a girl," she asked severely, "as long as it has the makes and the shapes of a Christian?"

John and I had the run of the Bridge Club with all its fascinating nooks and crannies. One day Mammy was working in our basement flat when she heard piercing screams coming from the top floor. She raced up the three flights of stairs with her breath in her fist, imagining disaster and no doubt muttering aspirations to an entire panoply of saints, only to find me calm and unhurt in one of the bedrooms. "Boy hit me," I told her by way of explanation. I called my brother by the generic Boy, because he was the only boy I knew and the center of my universe. Then there was the story of the Greedyguts. Before guests arrived to play bridge, Mammy laid out plates of biscuits with the fancy tea things. After the bridge players departed for the evening, John and I were allowed to go into the room to eat whatever biscuits they had left. More often than not, the plates were empty or held only a few crumbs for us. "They're Greedyguts," John said in disgust. One day a Bridge Club member came to the front door to see Mammy. John stuck his head out from behind her apron. "Is that one of the Greedyguts?" he asked.

Eventually my parents got a flat of their own in Rollins Villas, Sallynoggin, where the twins were born. But after only three months in Rollins Villas, Mammy and Dad were able to arrange a swap with another family and they moved into a real house at Number 4, Pearse Close, in September 1954. "It was the day after the All-Ireland Football Final," Dad recalled. "My brother came up from Trim and moved us with his lorry."

The houses in Pearse Close were rented to families with more than five children and the flats were usually occupied by people who were on a waiting-list for a house. Mrs. Dalton, who lived in one of the upper flats, had had to wait until she had five children before she got a house. That meant lugging the baby's pram, the other children, and all the messages up and down the flight of stone steps that led to her front door every time she went in or out. We had been lucky to get a house even though we were considered only a small family of six people.

Like all the houses in The Close, ours consisted of a small livingroom and sittingroom built back-to-back so as to accommodate a fireplace in both rooms. There was a tiny scullery off the livingroom and a hall that led to the front door. Mammy kept her cookbooks and cleaning supplies in the cupboard under the stairs, as well as her big purple chocolate box of family photos. She also kept apples in the cupboard, which gave it a sweet ripe smell. I loved to crouch inside the cupboard and close the door so that I could see my glow-in-the-dark statue of the Blessed Virgin Mary shine and pretend it was a vision from Heaven.

It seems to me now that I lived in a dream as a child. The fields of flowers where the tinkers or traveling people hung out their washing;

the bluebells that nodded in the fields in a falling wave; the cowslips that were lemon-colored like my Confirmation dress; the endless sweep of weeds that flourished in the neighbors' gardens; the heads of poppies that we picked apart to examine their embryonic, densely-colored hearts; the daisy-chains we made to decorate our dresses, to crown ourselves *Queen of the May*, to make ourselves beautiful—these were all part of my childhood landscape.

There were two bedrooms upstairs, one with a fireplace and the other with a hotpress next to the water heater, as well as a bathroom and a small attic space where Dad kept the Christmas decorations. Mammy and Dad had one bedroom, and the four of us—one boy and three girls—shared the other. Years later the tiny downstairs sittingroom was converted into a bedroom for John, in what I considered an act of the most appalling favoritism.

There was also a small front garden with a golden privet hedge and a larger back garden where Dad worked at the weekends and in the evenings when he wanted to get away from our squabbling and Mammy's incessant talking. The livingroom was dominated by the standard image of a singularly Aryan-looking Jesus holding out his Sacred Heart with its crown of thorns, set in a gilt frame. Later someone gave Dad an oil-painted portrait of the Irish patriot Robert Emmet, and he placed it on the wall to the right of The Sacred Heart. "Bold Robert Emmet, the darling of Erin," as the song said, had led a rebellion against the English in 1803. When the rebellion failed, as they all did, Emmet was captured and hanged, drawn and quartered in Thomas Street, Dublin. The Sacred Heart's melancholy brown eyes followed you around the livingroom, but Robert Emmet always seemed to be gazing raptly at the Sacred Heart himself, as if beseeching him for help.

The other two focal points in our house were the fireplace and the radio. Our house, like all the others, was made of cement blocks, and its only source of heat was the fireplace where we burned coal and turf. Dad loved a good fire so our livingroom was invariably scorching while the rest of the house was cold and dank. We took hot-water bottles to bed in the winter, but Dad would not allow us to have them at other times of year. He seemed to believe the calendar more than the actual temperature outside.

Hot-water bottles were a great comfort but they gave you chilblains on your toes that burned and throbbed and itched night and day. The torment of chilblains taught us that all comfort came with a big price-tag, a lesson that the teachings of the Catholic Church augmented, just in case we were in any doubt.

Chapter Nine

In those days, lower-income families like ours were given free tonics and nutritional supplements from the local dispensary. We were lucky to have the "white card" that provided free medical care, Mammy told us, although it was based on our lowly financial status. "The working poor," she called us, and "only poor working-class people." The tonics and energy boosters we consumed as children were only slightly removed from the snake-oil elixirs of the Victorian era, but we believed implicitly in whatever the government or the family doctor saw fit to bestow on us. Even the names of the elixirs had a convincing ring. There was "Retsel Brine Salts for gout, lumbago, rheumatism and sciatica," and "Trench's Remedy, a simple home treatment for fits and epilepsy."

Our Susan always had what the old people called "a dying look" as if she needed a good tonic. She was the smaller and skinnier of our twins and the baby of the family. The doctor recommended a special drink called "Parishes Food" to build up her blood. It came in a slender bottle and was a blood-red color, which gave it an authentic appearance. "Just like wine," Mammy said approvingly. We had seen the priest drink wine from the chalice but had never tasted such an exotic thing ourselves. Susan drank the stuff from a pink plastic eggcup, and I remember envying her this special treatment. Food—or the refusal of it—turned out to be the perfect weapon in my fight for attention. And it all started with cod liver oil and malt.

As far as I was concerned, my one and only brother John could do no wrong, so I didn't hesitate to follow his lead when he discovered the big brown jar of Cod Liver Oil & Malt, also recommended by the doctor, that Mammy had hidden in her bottom drawer in the bedroom. Armed with a silver tablespoon, John ladled out huge dollops of the sticky goo as we sat on the floor at the foot of her bed. Tucked up next to the brown jar among Mammy's silk slips and nightdresses was a smaller bottle labeled "Cherry Cough Mixture" and another entitled "Woodward's Gripe Water—for wind pains, teething and stomach upsets." "One for me and one for you," said John, and sometimes "two for me and one for you," as he spooned out the various liquids. It was my first experience of forbidden pleasure, my first inkling that there might be more to life than goodness and obedience, and I took to it like a duck to water. Mammy was horrified when she discovered us, sated but none the worse for wear, licking the last drops from our fingers. "Glory be to God and His Holy Mother!" she said. "I can't take my eyes off you for a minute."

Later, when I was old enough to be sent across the road to the shops for messages, I discovered that the fleshy middle of the soft "turnover" loaf of bread tasted better than the slices Mammy cut with the bread knife for toasting by the fire. And I couldn't resist sneaking a few slivers of the cooked corned beef that Baldy Brennan sliced and caught on a slip of greaseproof paper as they fell from the blade of his marvelous meat-cutting machine. I stuffed them into my mouth on the way home. Hadn't the forbidden apple of the Tree of Knowledge tasted better to Eve than all the other fruits in the Garden of Paradise?

I became a vegetarian less out of conviction and more out of a need to be different, and of course, to irritate Mammy. When it came to refusing meat, I backed myself into a corner and could never find the way out. It all began when I was eight and Dad came home from the country with a beautiful pheasant for our Sunday dinner. He often went home to go shooting with his brother John, who kept a shotgun and a legendary gun-dog named Jingles. When Dad got a pheasant, he would hang it on the back-door knob for a few days until he was ready to pluck and clean it. Our John loved this part of the process. He always had a scientific turn of mind and he was fascinated when Dad would pull his chair up to the fireplace, roll up his shirtsleeves, position the bird firmly between his knees, pluck the feathers from the skin with his strong hands, and throw them into the flames. When he opened up the bird's gizzard, Dad would show us what the pheasant had eaten for its last meal. I never liked the smell of burning feathers or the poor creature's forlorn look after Mammy had stuffed it with sage and breadcrumbs and trussed up its drumsticks with string.

One day I managed to unhook the pheasant, still dressed in its beautiful iridescent feathers, from where it was hanging on the doorknob. I laid it in my navy blue doll's pram, tucked the blankets around its beak, and took it for a walk around the street until Mammy caught me in the act. Having formed a relationship with the creature, I couldn't very well eat it and so declared myself a vegetarian from that point onward. The gesture drove Mammy up the walls, as I secretly hoped it would. "That girl is always putting on airs and graces," she fumed. I had found a weapon with which to torture her as well as a means of establishing a personal identity and nothing could dissuade me from my resolve. The family predicted ill health and an early death. Mammy said I was contrary as a bag of cats.

Though she didn't approve of my eating habits, Mammy pandered to the family's taste for sugar by baking cakes, puddings and pies galore. She always kept a tin of Lyle's Golden Syrup handy for making her wonderful golden toffee that could be chewed for hours or traded with other children at school in exchange for more exotic treats. One day when she had just finished cooking the toffee and had poured it into an enamel plate to cool on the table, I ran in from the street and reached out to touch it, expecting to encounter a hard, shiny surface. Instead, my fingers passed through the thin membrane into the boiling toffee underneath. I remember screaming, but the sound seemed to come from a great distance as if it was someone else's voice, someone else staring like King Midas at her suddenly gilded fingers. Mammy grabbed me and plunged my hand under the cold tap in the kitchen. In a matter of moments, neighbors appeared at the back door to find out who was being stabbed. Someone ran to the chemist's shop and returned with a tube of bright yellow ointment called "Burn-All." No one thought of calling a doctor. The toffee slid off in perfect finger-shaped molds, the "Burn-All" worked like a charm, and Mammy refused ever to make toffee again as long as she lived. It was all my fault for leaping before I looked, and for never cutting my garment according to my cloth, or so Mammy said regretfully.

She never got over fussing about my diet. When I turned into a rail-thin teenager, she theorized that I was deficient in the B vitamins, which I took to mean deficient in a larger spiritual sense. In my early twenties, I subsisted on cigarettes, coffee, and the dense brown bread that was sold at Bewley's Oriental Café in Dublin where I brooded for hours on poetry and existentialism. In retrospect, my broodiness was probably the result of ordinary starvation—the need for three squares a day.

Chapter Ten

I was initially a very devout child. I loved the idea of sainthood and had notions of depriving myself of food and becoming angelic and ethereal. I might well have achieved perfection, I always told myself, if it weren't for those infernal twins, my younger sisters. I nourished the selfish hope that something—I wasn't sure what—would happen to them, thereby restoring my world to the pre-twin paradise in which I had been the beloved and only girl.

Every class at Saint Joseph's primary school began and ended with prayers. One particularly cranky and terrifying teacher, Mrs. Crawford, made us say three "Hail Marys" every day for Holy Purity (whatever that was) and three more for The Conversion of Pagan England. Catholicism was full of the memorization and recitation of mysterious words and phrases. I could recite the names of the Seven Deadly Sins and the Seven Gifts of the Holy Ghost long before I knew the meaning of vice or virtue. I liked the sounds of words like "calumniate," "apostolic" and "incarnate," and I was good at memorizing prayers and poems. But what was a six-year-old to make of "covetousness" or "piety and the fear of the Lord"? I don't think it occurred to me to ask for explanations any more than it occurred to anyone to offer them.

The First Communion class nun told us that, if we could grasp what would happen to us when we received the body of Christ, we would all die on the spot. Hadn't Blessed Imelda expired instantly after receiving Communion from the hands of Our Lord? She had us on the verge of hysteria with fantasies of what would happen if we failed the Catechism test. Not only would Holy God weep but so would Our Lady, and worse still, we wouldn't get to make our First Communions. I had a vision of standing on the sidelines in disgrace while the First Communicants paraded around in their white dresses and veils, the picture of innocence, as they collected wads of money in their dainty purses. We had to dress in our best clothes and be on our best behavior the day that Father Martin, the local parish priest, was scheduled to come to the classroom to test our knowledge of the Catechism in preparation for our First Holy Communion. The nuns' awe of Father Martin was also a kind of awe of men in general, so that the kindly priest was unable to put us at ease with his jokes and smiles. As it turned out, it was not Father Martin but a bicycle accident that very nearly came between me and the sacrament.

In those days, no one we knew owned a telephone, a refrigerator, or a car, unless it was a delivery van like the one Dad drove for IMCO. Dad rode his bicycle to and from work and Mammy always carried the shopping home from Dun Laoghaire in a basket on the front of her big black bicycle. She often had one of us children riding behind her on the back carrier as well.

One evening I was riding with Mammy on her bicycle. It was getting on for twilight and the main road near our street was full of traffic. Somehow, I managed to get my foot stuck in the spokes of the bicycle's back wheel. The spoke bit into my ankle but my screams were drowned out by the noise of a double-decker bus that was passing by. The bike pitched over, fortunately not in the direction of the bus, and Mammy and I and the messages went flying. Mary Mac from next door saw the accident and obligingly ran home to tell Dad that I was dead.

There was a big fuss made over me and I was taken to St. Michael's hospital to have the ankle seen to. Illness and accident always garnered plenty of notice so, despite the pain, I reveled in the attention. Because she was not actually bleeding, no one gave Mammy any attention at all, although she was probably in worse shape than I was. As mother of the family, it was unthinkable that she would be laid up or take to her bed during daylight hours. There were two women on our street who disappeared periodically to Saint Brendan's, the mental asylum, but they were childless and therefore expendable. Their childlessness, the local gossips whispered, was part of the problem. But we could never do without Mammy. Hadn't we nearly perished when she had rheumatic fever? Her poor bike, the household's trusty carthorse, was fixed up and put back into service again. Every day for the better part of a year, I had to be taken to the outpatient clinic at the hospital to have my ankle treated and bandaged. It was all very fascinating except for one thing. Inside the front door of the hospital there was a terrifying sight—a great dark statue of Blessed Michael the Archangel brandishing a spear and attempting to crush a huge serpent with his sandaled foot. The foot and the serpent were directly at eye-level as I entered the door, and I tried hard not to look at them as I rushed past. The whole spectacle of statue, dreary corridor, and pale green tiles epitomized my fear that, once inside, anything could be done to me.

I made my First Holy Communion in Saint Michael's church, Dun Laoghaire, in May of that year. After the ceremony, I had to go to the hospital to have my ankle treated. But, ever the shoe fetishist, I managed to squeeze my bandaged foot into my white First Communion shoe for a couple of hours of public appearances.

When it came to Confirmation at age ten, the older kids warned us that the Archbishop of Dublin, John Charles McQuaid, was going to belt us across the face to make us soldiers of Christ. I felt weak with relief when I emerged from the church after the ceremony. Dr. McQuaid had only stroked my cheek and had helped with the Catechism questions. He asked me for the Seven Deadly Sins, and I managed to stammer them out in proper order. A new era had clearly dawned in Ireland's relationship with the Catholic Church when, a few years ago, my brother sent an Irish newspaper with the shocking headline: "Archbishop McQuaid – saint or pedophile?"

But when I was a child, no one thought to question the Church's rule. Each night at home, Mammy stood in our bedroom doorway and made the sign of the cross over us with holy water before we went to sleep. We dipped our fingers in the holy water font inside our own front door and made the sign of the cross as we entered and left the house. When we swam in the teeth-chattering Irish Sea, we blessed ourselves with seawater to prevent drowning. And when the altar-boy rang the bell during Benediction on Sunday afternoons and the priest held up the host and recited the sacred words, we fell to our knees and bent our heads, as if attached by puppet-strings to the glittering monstrance. These were the comforting everyday rituals of our lives.

Still, I felt the need for a secret life in a world that gave short shrift to privacy and discouraged children from "getting notions" about themselves. For a time I became heavily religious, reading the lives of the saints, gathering cowslips and primroses for May altars to the Virgin, and hand-coloring garish statues of the Sacred Heart for relatives. I thought I could see visions in a *Penny Luckybag* ring if I held my hand so it caught the light from the stained-glass windows of the church. Wouldn't it be romantic, I mused, to be singled out by God for a life of virtue and then, when you died at an early age, to send down showers of roses so your friends and relations could marvel and rejoice? I took Therese for my Confirmation name in memory of The Little Flower of Avila, though I secretly hoped that God would not decide to call me to the religious life. The nuns were clear on that subject. If God called you, you had better come running or resign yourself to a life of shame and selfishness. I prayed He would look the other way.

Everything, including religion, was magical to me then. I was always looking for mysteries. The Little Armchair Rock at the seafront was just big enough to hold me and I believed I was hidden from other people's eyes when I sat there. The bright orange nasturtiums on the railway bank were secret flowers that hid beneath their leaves and only I could discover them.

There were weekend retreats at the school convent that involved long periods of mandatory silence. We slept on narrow beds separated by chintz curtains in the convent dormitory. Each cubicle had a pitcher of cold water and an enamel basin for washing. The weekend began with Confession, followed by a resolution to turn over a new leaf and sin no more. Sunday, the last day of the Retreat, was supposed to be the culmination of our sanctity. Tea was served in the dining room. A nun read to us from a religious book while we ate. There were miraculously thin slices of bread, small glass bowls of jam, and exquisite curls of butter on the table. But I sought in vain for that virtuous glow, knowing I was guilty of wanting to be "special," and of trying to trick God and my parents into loving me more than my sisters.

Chapter Eleven

The Daughters of the Heart of Mary ran St. Joseph's primary school on Tivoli Road as well as the orphanage where the twins had stayed during Mammy's bout with rheumatic fever. Out of loyalty to the nuns, my parents sent us to school there instead of the Harold National School in Glasthule where Mammy had gone to school herself. The Daughters dressed in civilian clothes instead of full-length black habits in order to blend in with the people they served at home or on the foreign missions. The only problem was that their hairstyles and clothes—ladies' tweed "costumes" of the nineteen-forties—did not change with the fashion, so they were immediately recognizable to one and all as nuns.

Every morning school began with the ritual of filling the inkwells. The teacher's pet was deputized to carry out the task. She poured the deep blue liquid from a china jug into the small white porcelain cups and delivered them on a tray to our desks with the air of an acolyte distributing the blood of the Savior. We placed the inkwells in the receptacles in the upper right-hand corner of our desks and dipped the day away with our wooden-handled pens, practicing flowery scripts in "headline" copybooks. The metal nib bit into the side of my finger. I have the indentation still. I was afraid of the nuns and the other children, afraid to speak or move, able only to do what I was told—keep my head down, practice my letters, and try to avoid getting into trouble with the nuns. Worst of all would be being slapped with a ruler in front of the whole class.

Cookery class was by far the worst three hours of the week. I had no confidence in the kitchen and no taste for the dishes the nuns deemed appropriate for our future lives as mothers and housewives—fish dishes and forcemeats for dinner, milk puddings and possets for dessert, and beef tea and junket for invalids. Although Mammy was a good cook, she had neither the time nor the patience to allow me to ruin her expensive ingredients by teaching me to cook herself. We were already rivals for Dad's attention and she was not about to let me sabotage her role as steward of his pronounced sweet tooth. I had always been a finicky eater and, since the age of eight, a confirmed vegetarian. The nuns gave short shrift to such pretensions. Neither were they impressed by modern conveniences like powdered mixes or readymade sauces. We cooked in pairs, with one girl in charge of the cooking while the other fetched and carried and acted as her helper. I prayed to be chosen as helper when we cleaned and cooked a stuffed sheep's heart, but my prayers went unanswered. I recoiled likewise at the marmalade pudding made with suet, and the custard that refused to lose its lumps. Poor Dad, obliged to sample these culinary disasters when we brought them home from school, was lavish with his compliments. But even he would sometimes recall our grandfather's dictum: "There's no doubt about it," he used to say, "God made the food but the Divil made the cooks!"

Scholarly achievement depended on the weekly spelling test. If you got twenty out of twenty spellings correct, you got to sit in the front row of the classroom. Children who could not spell anything right were put in the back row. With more than fifty children to one teacher, it was no wonder some were simply ignored. I was a good speller so I was always at the front of the class. Unfortunately, my twin sisters could not seem to learn how to spell. The word "dyslexia" was unknown, as was the notion of different methods of teaching and learning. An inability to spell was considered mere laziness. I was always being called into the twins' classroom to be presented as a model student, and then instructed to go home and teach my sisters their spellings. I failed miserably at this task, and my attempts did nothing to improve relations with my sisters.

I was not surprised one day when Miss Holmes called me out of the classroom into the hall. She beckoned me over to stand in front of her. I glanced around. All the doors were shut and the hall was empty. Miss Holmes, who was dressed in a no-nonsense brown tweed costume with sensible brown-laced shoes, glared down at me from above. "Angela Goggins," she said, "do you know that your neck is black?" I was flabbergasted. No one had ever said such a thing to me before. "What would your Mammy say if she could see you?" she went on. "Go home and wash your neck and don't come to school like that again." I had never felt so ashamed in all my life.

That night I went into the bathroom and looked at myself in the little mirror on the front of the shaving cabinet. Sure enough, there was a ring of dirt all around the back of my neck. I washed myself as best I could but I could not wash away the embarrassment or the feeling of impending doom the incident had left behind. In my innocence and ignorance, I had not noticed something so obvious as my own lack of cleanliness. What else might I have overlooked? How was I supposed to know what was coming or how to prepare for it? Mammy made us wash our faces and hands but she was too busy to pay attention to the rest. During the summer, we swam in the sea every day so we stayed relatively clean, but the rest of the year was hit or miss.

Mammy was a great cook and a wonderful storyteller but, as a housekeeper, she couldn't seem to get organized. She was always late for everything. On Sunday mornings, Dad inspected us before we went to Mass. "Why aren't this child's shoes polished?" he'd demand, or "Does she not have anything better to wear?" Mammy was always rushing out the door as the final bell was ringing while Dad strode on ahead, determined to be on time for Mass. "You'd think he didn't want to be seen with us," she complained furiously as she panted up the road, clutching her handbag with one hand and trying to tie her headscarf with the other.

Chapter Twelve

I never knew Dad had only one eye until the day he sat the four of us children down and told us his secret, although as we discovered later, it was only part of the story. He had been poked in the eye with a sharp stick when he was at school, he said, and after years of trouble, the eye was removed and a glass one put in its place.

We were gob-smacked. I stared at Dad's familiar face, amazed that I had never noticed how the right eye didn't move, although now its immobility seemed as obvious as the nose on his face or the cleft in his chin. Why hadn't he told us before now, we wanted to know. "I was afraid you'd go and tell the neighbors," Dad said, "and I'd lose my job as a van-driver if they found out I had only one eye. And then where would we be?"

We got the picture. Dad worked for a dry-cleaning firm called IMCO, the Invisible Mending Company, in Merrion, County Dublin. He bicycled five miles to work and then spent his days "dealing with oulwans," as he put it, driving all over the city, picking up and delivering clothes to the various IMCO shops. He was always instructing us to avoid talking to the neighbors. "I don't want people gossiping about how much money I earn or what I do for a living," he said. "Don't be making a holy show of yourselves telling my business to strangers."

The command to desist from making a holy show of yourself was issued whenever you were seen to be putting yourself forward or attracting notice in public. I was painfully shy and yet also desperate for attention, an unfortunate combination of character traits that guaranteed a rich interior life and a truly miserable childhood.

I fell in love with reading at an early age because I lacked even the most basic social skills. The outside world was terrifying and

Mammy let us know she was reluctant to push us into it before our time. I didn't go to school until I was five and a half, and it was just as frightening as I had been led to expect. I was afraid not to be good, and I followed the rules to avoid scrutiny.

But praise was what I wanted most at home. I was always a Daddy's girl, consumed with the desire to win his attention away from the others. I spent hours learning poems to recite to him after he had had his dinner and was sitting at the table over his tea and a bit of Mammy's sweet cake. "The gingham dog and the calico cat/side by side on the table sat," I'd declaim, holding out my skirts in demure little-girl fashion. "You don't know what she's been up to while you were gone," Mammy would mutter disparagingly in the background. "She has no sense of the fitness of things." Dad was deaf to such remarks. When it came to language and "speaking nicely," he was a terrific snob.

Our John, who was two years older than I, was a saint, the white-headed, only boy of the family. A born peacemaker, he arbitrated as best he could during my bitter arguments with Mary and Susan, the twins, who were two years younger than I was. I always demanded privileges as the oldest daughter, but my parents were wise enough to ignore my entreaties. "We would never make fish of one and flesh of another," they said firmly.

All of Mammy's talking, although entertaining, had the effect of turning me into a quiet, bashful child and later a painfully shy young woman. I retreated to the private sanctuary of books to shut out the racket that went on all around me. Books were also an escape from the realities of nuns, teachers, and other children. I infinitely preferred diving into the lives of Jo March, Katie Carr, and Anne of Green Gables to dealing with the bossy girls outside or standing up to the boys who chased us home from school with nettles wrapped in newspaper.

I loved the books that were serialized on Radio Eireann—*Journey to the Center of the Earth* and *Twenty Thousand Leagues Under The Sea*. I devoured John's stories about Davy Crockett and King Arthur and the Knights of the Round Table. Most of all, I lived for the weekly English comics, *Bunty* and *Judy*, that I got across the road at the newsagents that was also the post office and the sweetshop. I followed the story of "Sandra and the Secret Ballet," about a poor child who was kidnapped and taken to a remote island by an embittered, crippled ballerina to be trained for a future at Sadler's Wells. There was also a story about a sweet-faced girl who struggled to maintain her virtue while keeping her countless siblings out of the Workhouse.

Our John got *The Beezer* and *The Beano* but he was just as eager for the girls' "to be continued" serials as I. Likewise, I was inspired by a story in John's boys' adventure annual about two English children who went to Australia. The boy, David, was terrified of the ocean but managed to save his sister from a shark. Of course, I assumed that David was John and I was the adored sister. I could easily imagine the hot white beach and the bronzed lifeguard who befriended the children. The newsagent also sold *Marvel* comics and "45 Pagers," the English war comics that featured square-headed "Krauts" and "slanty-eyed Japs" who were always defeated by tall, lean, lantern-jawed, morally-upstanding British or Australian officers. "Oul' comicuts," our neighbor Mrs. Fitzgerald called our beloved comics disparagingly. But they captured our imaginations and made us avid readers before television had time to gain a toehold. We looked forward to the "folley-up" stories from week to week, just like Charles Dickens' fans or the husband of Scheherazade in *The Arabian Nights*.

From the comics I moved on to the children's library, a small prefabricated building around the back of the red-brick adult Carnegie Library on Lower George's Street in Dun Laoghaire. I started with books about horses, including *Jill at the Gymkhana*, *Jill and Black Boy*, and the intriguingly titled *Jill Enjoys Her Ponies*. (How mortified I felt years later when my American father-in-law remarked on the Freudian implications of young girls' fascination with horses.) There was also a series of ballet stories that followed the adventures of *Lorna at Sadler's Wells*. Then I began trading books with my cousin Betty.

Together we devoured *First-through-Sixth Form at Malory Towers* by Enid Blyton and other stories of British boarding-school life. One of these stories featured Patti, who was, in retrospect, a sickeningly good child. Patti had won a scholarship to an expensive boarding school and the first chapter found her packing her school trunk while her mother doled out tender advice on morals, etiquette, and general good behavior. In one memorable episode, Patti faced the dreadful dilemma of possessing only two shillings with which to buy Christmas gifts for her twelve little brothers and sisters at home. Another boarding school saga introduced Roberta, familiarly known as Bobby. I loved the descriptions of her large colorful family who lived in a large colorful house festooned with climbing roses, drenched in sunshine, and set in the English countryside. I knew that I would be a better person in the bosom of Bobby's family, who would no doubt appreciate me more than my own ungrateful parents and siblings.

Mammy and Aunt Kathleen loved to swap romantic novels and, in my early teens, I read all of them as soon as they came my way. I relished the lavish descriptions of clothes and finery in Georgette Heyer's Regency romances. For a while, I even took up the habit of taking snuff from a little tin box, à la Beau Brummel. Mammy just shook her head at my affectations. Annie M.P. Smithson's Irish novels appealed to me because of their religious-patriotic zeal. Smithson's heroines were always falling in love with Protestants, then having visions of the Blessed Virgin in the nick of time before they threw away their immortal souls, and entering convents where they lived lives of saintly purity while offering up prayers for the conversion of their former lovers.

For my sixteenth birthday, Aunt Kathleen gave me a set of Penguin paperbacks, the short stories of Somerset Maugham, Volumes 1, 2 and 3. These marked a turning point in my reading life, my discovery of "literature" as opposed to my indiscriminate absorption of narrative and plot.

It was a proud day when I graduated to the adult library and could carry home hard-backed volumes like Dickens' *Nicholas Nickelby*, Whitman's *Leaves of Grass*, and the plays of Eugene O'Neill, although I mostly did it to impress Mammy and to resist her advice to "go out and play in the fresh air and not be ruining your lovely eyes with reading all those depressing books." I had never heard of F. Scott Fitzgerald, but Bob Dylan mentioned him in a song and nothing would do me but to look him up, whoever he was.

Chapter Thirteen

When Christmas came, we thanked our lucky stars we had grown up in Dublin and not in County Meath like Dad. At his home, they always killed a pig at Christmas. The children were sent off to gather holly, better still if it had red berries on it. "But we heard the pig screaming anyway," Dad said. To us city children, the Christmas tree signaled the start of the festive season. Dad kept us waiting until it seemed that every other family in Ireland had a tree blinking and twinkling in its sittingroom window. Just as we despaired of ever getting ours up in time, he would arrive home on his bicycle, carrying the tree over his shoulder. He and Mammy would discuss the shocking cost of Christmas trees and the haggling that had taken place over this one. We didn't care. We were enchanted by the smell of pine that seemed to transform our little Corporation house into a strange and wonderful abode.

My sisters and I lusted after dolls. We stood for hours with our noses pressed to the window of Mrs. Grace's toyshop in Dun Laoghaire, picking out the exact ones we wanted for Christmas. We firmly believed that Santa Claus knew just which doll belonged to which child and would bring them to us for Christmas just as surely as we knew the sun would rise, that God was good, and that our parents loved us (although being reticent Irish people, they rarely mentioned that fact).

Then there was the elaborate ritual of the Christmas cake, which was supposed to be made several months in advance to give it time to absorb the flavors of the whiskey or brandy with which it was laced. Because Mammy was perpetually late with everything, the Christmas cake was always thrown together in a panic at the last minute. In the evening, Aunt Kathleen arrived at our house armed with the tools of the cake-decorating trade. She expertly sheathed the cake in almond paste, followed by a layer of Royal icing that was white as a snowstorm and hard as the knocker of Newgate.

In the days before Christmas, Uncle Des rode his bicycle across the Swan's Hollow from Dalkey, bringing a big tin of biscuits for the family. He worked as Clerk of Dalkey parish church. Although he was a father of six, I always thought him rather saintly with his black suit and the bicycle clips that kept his trouser-legs free of oil and grease. Uncle Willie came up from County Meath with fresh eggs and a sack of coal. He was large, red-faced, and genial. A half-dozen children followed in his wake. Our cousins. They peered at us from behind Uncle Willie's broad back. With their large frightened eyes, they looked like a herd of half-wild bullocks prepared to bolt at sudden movements. On the afternoon of Christmas Day, Uncle Christy came to visit us with "the lassies," as he liked to refer to our girl cousins, Betty and Helen, and Pat, who, because he was a boy, merited the entire category of "Son" all to himself.

On Christmas Eve, we borrowed Dad's socks and fastened one to the foot of each of our beds. Since there were only two small bedrooms in the house, the four of us children shared a room for years. First thing on Christmas morning, we dived for the ends of our beds with shouts of glee and tore into the bulging stockings. We firmly believed that the English sweets we loved were specially made at the North Pole; in fact, Dad's two sisters, who were nurses in Somerset, had sent them. There was always an orange in our stockings and, right in the toe, a shiny copper penny.

Apart from the dolls, there were hula hoops and roller-skates, a silver-and-white Lone Ranger rifle for John, and paint-boxes whose tiny squares of color had delicious names like Titanium Red, Burnt Umber and Yellow Ochre. Christmas also brought hardcover "annuals" based on the weekly English comics we adored—"Bunty," "Judy," and "The Beano."

I remember one Christmas in particular. On the afternoon of

Saint Stephen's Day (December 26), we set off for our usual visit to Aunt Nancy and Uncle Christy's house, about a mile up the road. I thought Aunt Nancy's house much grander than ours, although it was a similarly simple Corporation house, built in the 1940s. Perhaps it was the large front garden or, most impressive of all, the toilet with its own special room separated from the bath. Aunt Nancy met us at the door with kisses, wishing us "Happy Christmas" in her wonderful raspy voice, the result of years of cigarette smoking. When she smiled, which she always did, the skin around her eyes crinkled up like parchment as if it too had been smoked from years of sitting in her favorite chair by the fireplace.

There were butterfly cakes filled with cream in the kitchen, and a glass case filled with china in the livingroom. We played hide-and-seek with our cousins, although we were forbidden to jump on the beds as we did in our house. Everyone had to be quiet for the football results on television. At teatime Uncle Christy, who was a sailor, amused us all with his nautical expressions. "Sing out now," he'd call as he poured the tea, "and somebody close the porthole in the galley." There were English Christmas crackers by our plates and thin slices of Aunt Nancy's Christmas cake.

When it was time to leave, we pulled on hats and coats, said our farewells, and opened the front door. Then, what joy! The whole world covered in snow and not another child in the neighborhood awake to spoil it. We were ecstatic – the Chosen Family. We walked home in great excitement, stopping every few yards to exclaim at the patterns our shoes made in the snow. Even the little hucksters' shops we passed had a fairytale quality, all meanness hidden under a mantle of white. When we got to our street, John and I rolled a snowball so big we couldn't squeeze it through our garden gate. Next morning all the beautiful snow had turned to slush under the neighbors' footsteps. But we were satisfied, knowing we had been singled out by God for special treatment.

Chapter Fourteen

As we crossed the Vermont state line into Massachusetts, I wondered what the people at my office would think when I didn't show up after lunch. How long would it be before it occurred to anyone to ask where I was? I was one of three secretaries in the University's Department of Developmental Disabilities. We sat, one behind the other, like the *Bord Gáis* bears, in the long, dismal hallway of an old building. From time to time, the men in the offices would emerge and give one of us some handwritten notes to type on our electric "golfball" typewriters. Men had always been kind to me and these men were no exception, but I despised the menial role of secretary. It was just an extension of my lifelong tendency to go along with what men wanted because I had no idea what I wanted myself, and then I'd resent them for failing to make me happy.

What I had always wanted was an intellectual life—it was clearly the only thing I was fit for—and the job allowed me to take some free university courses before I committed to becoming a full-time English major, part-time secretary, and single mother. I had no idea of college requirements or grades, and I knew nothing of study habits and techniques. But I had always been in love with words and ideas. Hadn't I propped up my copy of *Great Expectations* on the eye-level grill when I was cooking baby-food back in Dublin? I always had bits of poetry running through my head like a river. "The curfew tolls the knell of parting day," I'd repeat to myself, loving Gray's rolling rhythms. "What are days for? /Days are where we live," I'd remind myself when morning made me want to curl up in a fetal position and go back to sleep. "The moan of doves in immemorial elms, and murmuring of innumerable bees"—the sound of Tennyson admonishing some anonymous maid to climb down from her high horse was a surreptitious pleasure, like sucking a gob-stopper when your mother's back was turned. I longed for a life of the mind, the freedom to float above the everyday, examine it from afar. What I really needed was a life of the body—a lusty laying on of hands—but that would not happen for some considerable time.

Meanwhile, I discovered that I possessed a kind of doggedness that would allow me to keep going. Although I had formed some strong friendships during the years in Milton and Winooski, I still felt as if I always had one foot out the door. I kept writing cheerful letters home, full of bits of news and weather—my son's precocious vocabulary, his marks at school, and my first awkward attempts at cross-country skiing in Vermont's snowy woods and fields. While not entirely fiction, those letters were undoubtedly marvels of omission and imagination. I almost believed them myself at times.

Now here I was, locked into this lemon of a car, with nothing but poetry and *plamás* to protect me from a gun-toting madman whose hands kept twitching on the steering-wheel. I wondered if he was "on" something, but there was no way to know. I sat there clutching my book-bag, my back pressed into the passenger seat, and tried to think what to do.

Chapter Fifteen

The men who came to our house to play music with Dad were "characters." Most of them were employed as bus-drivers and conductors by C.I.E., the Irish transportation company. I was fascinated by their foibles, facial tics, and malapropisms. I watched them intently, the better to make fun of them later on. Tom Keogh was a bus-driver and a diabetic. He had snow-white hair and pink eyes and he played the fiddle. As the evening wore on and our little livingroom began to throb with heat, Mr. Keogh would put down his fiddle, push his chair into the far corner of the room, and draw out a huge white handkerchief to polish the sweat from his high forehead.

Matt Ward, a bus-driver on the 45A route, played the accordion. He was short and round and he always stared at the ceiling as he squeezed the music-box. We spent hours examining his neck and chin, stockpiling remarks to be shared after the visitors went home. John-Joe Kelley hailed from Roscommon. "Good woman, good woman," he called out to Mammy when she served the tea and biscuits. Willie Hickey was a drummer and the leader of "The Silver Spear Ceili Band" that Dad belonged to for several years. I thought Willie Hickey was lovely with his oily black curls and blue eyes. But Dad thought his drums drowned out the fiddles, and Willie's sense of showmanship was at odds with Dad's more serious attitude to music and to life in general.

There was Matt Kane who had a habit of repeating, "Now do you understand me? Now do you know what I mean?" in the course of his conversation. Sometimes he came to call on Dad at the weekends. We'd wait for him to utter his signature phrase and would hardly be able to contain ourselves until the front door closed and we could imitate his facial expressions and intonations, much to our parents' amusement.

Banished to bed on musical nights, my sisters and I clustered on the stairs in our long flannel nightdresses like moths drawn to the light and heat of the livingroom. I noticed the way the men tucked their chins into their fiddles and tapped their feet in unison, swinging smoothly from tune to tune as if in the sway of a tribal drift. They knew hundreds of tunes by ear and the names of the tunes reflected the rhythms of Irish speech: "When Sick Is It Tay You Want?," "On A Morning of Sweet Recreation," "Round The House and Mind the Dresser," and "Take Me Now While I'm In Humor." Though I didn't know it at the time, the habit of sitting quietly on the sidelines, observing other people and eavesdropping on their conversations, would stand me in good stead as a writer later on.

The Meaghers were regular visitors to the music sessions at our house. The entire Meagher family was involved in Irish music. Mr. and Mrs. Meagher went to all the sessions with their six children. The eldest, Jerry, played the piano-accordion and his wife Camilla went with him everywhere. Jerry's brother Pat played the fiddle, Terry played the drums, Aidan another fiddle, Tony the whistle, and their sister Mary danced. She had long black ringlets – the perfect little Irish girl. We liked the Meaghers but I remember thinking that Dad must have been deeply disappointed in us by comparison.

Then there was Bob Rainey from Ballymena, a fiddle-playing bus-driver and a great friend of Dad's whom he visited once or twice in the North of Ireland. After one of his visits, Dad described the "black Freemasons" of the North who hated Catholics and even put padlocks on the playground gates on Sundays. This, above all, was held as proof of the mean-spiritedness of the North and seemed to explain perfectly eight hundred years of enmity between our two cultures.

Chapter Sixteen

The cul-de-sac at Pearse Close was a theatre-in-the-round, full of characters who played out the dramas of their lives within earshot of their neighbors. They were our chief source of amusement. We entertained ourselves by imitating their figures of speech and making fun of their malapropisms. I don't think it occurred to us that we were unkind or uncharitable. We had a fine sense of our own closeness as a family and enjoyed thinking ourselves better than the rest. In the top flat two doors down from us was Mrs. Hughes. She wore a pink plastic eyeshade over one eye with a rubber band around the back of her head to hold it in place. Every summer, her two grandchildren, Margaret and Johnny, came from London to stay with her. Although we were particularly impressed with Americans, we were fascinated with foreignness in general and Londoners were different and foreign enough. Our John had a crush on Margaret and I had a crush on Johnny because of their Cockney accents. "A cup o' tea and a hang sangwidge," John and I would repeat to each other when we went home to our own house after spending the afternoon with Johnny and Margaret. One day when John was giving Margaret Hughes a crossbar on his bicycle, he crashed into the wall at the bottom of The Close. Margaret escaped unscathed but John's knee swelled up to three times its size and he was taken away in the ambulance to Loughlinstown Hospital. I always considered him a victim of the romance of the spoken word.

In Number 3, the house next door to us, lived the O'Connors. Mr. O'Connor was a baggage handler at Dublin Airport. He used to catch conger eels off the West Pier and bring them home tied to the crossbar of his bike with their tails flapping in the wind. Mrs. O'Connor was thin and mysterious-looking. She always wore black and had a hat with a spotted veil that covered her face. Mary, the eldest O'Connor child, was only a little older than I was but she had a knowing look. "An oul' granny," Mammy called her when she heard that Mary was trying to teach me about the so-called facts of life. "That one knows more than her prayers," my parents said. They needn't have worried. I understood almost nothing of what Mary O'Connor told me about blood and your monthly "friends" and where babies came from. However, my need to pretend I did understand ensured that my ignorance would be profound and long lasting.

In the downstairs flat next door to us were the MacDonalds. Mrs. Mac was a hypochondriac who invented obscure illnesses. At times, she suffered from a mysterious "dropped stomach," which was probably a prolapsed womb, and at other times, she had trouble with her "bronnicles." She was painfully thin and always looked pinched with the cold. She wore her hair in tight curlers all week except on Sundays when she took out the curlers and covered her head in a chiffon scarf to go to Mass. Willie Mac had red hair and sandy eyebrows. Whenever you asked him what he was making out of the bits of old bicycles and scrap metal pieces he kept in his yard, he'd say, "I'm making a hen-house for a cat!" He loved children but could not get on with his wife. "Scorpio and Sagittarius are very unsuitable," Mammy said when we heard Mr. and Mrs. Mac arguing over the back wall while we were having our tea. Mammy always tried to put a good spin on things, as if it was her duty to shield us from all unpleasant emotions, including our own. Mrs. Mac had a special devotion to Blessed Martin De Porres, a Dominican priest who was born in Lima, Peru, in 1579. She was determined to get him canonized and she collected pennies for his cause in a little box with a penny-slot and a pop-up picture of a black man with sad brown eyes and kinky hair on the lid. Pope John XXIII canonized Blessed Martin in 1962, and Mrs. Mac should have been sainted too for her efforts on his behalf.

When it came to the saints, we all knew that Saint Anthony would help you find anything that was lost and Saint Christopher would protect you when you were traveling. Mammy taught us a prayer that we prattled every morning: "Holy Saint Christopher, God bless Daddy in the IMCO van, Amen." For general protection, Mammy draped us in brown and purple scapulars that we wore underneath our clothes. These were small brown squares of specially-blessed cloth connected by a ribbon around your neck so that one square lay on your chest and the other between your shoulder-blades. We carried small silver-and-blue miraculous medals to save us in dire extremity. Saint Jude was the patron saint of lost causes. The nuns gathered all the pupils in the assembly hall at school for a prayer to Saint Jude before they sat for their exams. When we paid a visit to the church, Mammy always knelt before the statue of Saint Anne, her patron saint, the mother of John the Baptist and the patron saint of all mothers and housewives, knowing that there at least she would find a sympathetic ear for her troubles.

When it came to running errands for grown-ups, any child on the street was fair game. Mrs. Weir, who lived upstairs over the MacDonalds, would beckon you from the top window. "Will you go across the road and get me a few messages?" she'd say. "Five cigarettes, a bottle of milk, and a half stone of coal." The shopkeeper would open a packet of ten *Players Navy Cut*, take out five cigarettes, wrap them in brown tissue paper, and then fold up the remaining cigarettes to be sold in ones and twos to corner-boys later on. If you were lucky, Mrs. Weir would tell you to keep the penny for yourself after you had hauled the messages up the steps to her flat. The Mulligans lived in Number 10, and had two daughters, Mary and Pat, and a son called Eamon who was friendly with our John. It was rumored that Mr. Mulligan, a bus-driver who had been in the military, would not allow Eamon to touch the dishes or do any housework. Mr. Mulligan taught boxing to the local lads and I often saw him coming home from the pub in the evening, his military bearing a little askew so that he leaned stiffly back on his heels, his head erect and his broad boxer's chest thrust forward to lead the way.

In addition to boxing lessons, there were tap-dancing classes offered in the neighborhood. I got as far as the door one time, but I was too shy and self-conscious to go in to the dancing class. Bernie Weir's cousin, Marie Aylward, was a periodic visitor to our street. She was a pretty child with curly hair, who fancied herself a singer and tap-dancer. We were her captive audience, sitting in a line on the little wall at the edge of the green while she performed songs from popular musicals. "I Could Have Danced All Night," she'd sing, holding her skirt out in a curtsey at the end of the number. I wondered what it was like to be so pretty and confident. "Don't be putting yourself forward," we were told, "and when in doubt, say nowt."

The Phelans lived in Number 19, on the lower end of Pearse Close, and had a girl named Marie who was my own age. I bitterly envied her long, thick red hair. In our house, my sisters and I pulled Mammy's nylon stockings over our heads and left the legs hanging down, pretending we had long hair to toss around our shoulders like Marie Phelan. Mammy refused to let us grow our hair long on the grounds that we didn't have "nice" hair, by which she meant those bouncy ringlets favored by Irish dancers. The real reason was the outbreaks of lice that went around our street and school. Mammy spent evening after evening fine-combing our heads over sheets of newspaper on the kitchen floor, and the soft clink of nits hitting the paper is as unforgettable as the smell of "Sulio," the special lotion she put in our hair to discourage infestations.

Then there were the Kanes around the other corner of The Close, facing the main road. In a Catholic country with no divorce, no abortion, and no contraception except for the Church's concession to the ridiculous "rhythm method," there was no legal recourse for women whose husbands had deserted them. We knew several cases in which the husband had skipped it to England and was never heard from again. Nevertheless, mothers were expected to stay at home and bring up their children rather than go to work outside the home. In the Kane household, there was no Mr. Kane, and Mrs. Kane was obliged to leave her two sons, Terry and Tony, at home alone all day while she went out to work. The boys were reputed to be wild and uncivilized. One day Dad found Terry Kane in our backyard stealing apples. He thought nothing of boxing the younglad's ears and threatening him with worse if he ever caught him near our place again. That evening as we were having our tea, we heard a commotion outside. There was Mrs. Kane standing in the street outside our house with her sleeves rolled up, shouting abuse at Dad at the top of her voice. I couldn't believe that she had the nerve to speak to our stern upstanding father that way. "If you touch my Terry again, I'll have the law on you," she screamed as all the neighbors looked on from behind their lace-curtained windows. Dad was utterly mortified, not because he had beaten Terry Kane, but because Mrs. Kane had embarrassed him in front of the neighbors. "Those younglads are divils, both of them," he said, "and their mother is a terrible termagant. She has a tongue that would clip hedges."

Chapter Seventeen

Pearse Close was a cul-de-sac of twenty concrete-block houses that faced each other, with a green in the middle where all the children played. At the bottom of our cul-de-sac was a main street with two factories—Stroud-Reilly where nylon stockings were produced, and Kapp & Peterson, the smoking-pipe makers. The double-decker bus trundled past, along with the occasional car. In case of emergencies, there was a telephone kiosk down the road. When you went inside and closed the door, the smell of cigarettes made your eyes smart. Pearse Close was protected by a low stonewall at the open end of the cul-de-sac that served as a football goal and a theatrical stage as well as a blockade when marauding tribes of Corcorans and Breens came down from the rival neighborhoods of Pearse Park and Pearse Road to pelt us with stones. "Youse weren't brought up, youse were dragged up," they would yell, and we'd fire our stones at them from behind the wall.

Every few years Dun Laoghaire Corporation sent a squad of painters to refurbish the front doors, windowsills, and railings of Pearse Close with whatever colors they chose to paint them. Some years all the houses would be yellow, other years pale blue. But the coming of the painters was always an occasion. They were paid for "wet time," and because it rained almost every day, the process of painting the houses could be stretched out indefinitely. "Ah sure, it'll be there after you," the painters said when anyone expressed concern over the length of time the job was taking. "Sure Rome wasn't built in a day." The painters usually got a housewife to boil a kettle of water so they could make tea in a billy-can with the sugar and milk all stirred in together. They often holed up in our shed, drinking tea and playing cards by the hour while a younglad was dispatched to the corner to look out for the foreman in case he arrived to supervise the work.

At the top of the road stood Our Lady of Victories church. Like a medieval monastery, the church visually dominated the landscape and its bells summoned the faithful to Mass on Sundays and holidays. At either end of our road were rows of shops. The lower shops included Smiths, which sold sweets and ice-pops and housed the post office where women picked up their monthly Children's Allowance money and children bought savings stamps. You stuck the stamps in a book and waited until they had mounted up to a fortune. "Look after the pennies and the pounds will look after themselves," the neighbors used to say. I was never any good at saving, having no sense of the future—a character flaw that continues to this day—and I always cashed in my stamps before they could amount to anything worthwhile.

Betty Carey owned Honeypark Dairy. There were no refrigerators in those days, so we went to Betty Carey's for a block of ice cream to go with the jelly after our Sunday dinner. It was the local gossip shop and there was always a group of women in headscarves clustered inside. "Tell your Mammy this and tell your Mammy that," Betty would say to the children of her particular confidantes. She was very nosey but she always knew when the next 7A bus was due to come flying down from the terminus and round the corner in front of her shop.

The shops at the upper end of our road were known as "The Top Shops" and they included Mr. Jacko Jackinelli's fish and chip shop, where everyone spoke Italian and we got ice-cream cones with raspberry cordial on Sunday mornings after Mass, a reward for sitting through the interminable service and not asking "Daddy, when will Mass be over?" more than once every five minutes. Coyne's, the butcher's, had long wooden tables, sawdust on the floor, and a big cooler room in the back in which you could see the carcasses of animals hanging up on hooks. Brown's the Chemist was dark and quiet, a center of medical assistance. In those days, no one thought of calling a doctor unless they were at death's door, and the chemist was relied on for all the accidents, ailments, and the myriad catastrophes that flesh was heir to. Women brought their prams to the shops, not only to transport their children, but also to carry home the week's messages, and as often as not, a sack of spuds and a bale of briquettes as well.

"The shops in Sallynoggin are only hucksters' shops," Mammy said disparagingly. She rode her bicycle up and down the Noggin Hill to Dun Laoghaire to do the shopping at McGovern's, the grocers, where she had worked as a shop assistant before she was married and everyone knew her as Annie Swords. I loved McGovern's. It had wooden floors and a row of stools that you could climb on to reach the counter. There were long rolls of brown paper and twine for tying packages. Bird Swords, the bookkeeper (who was no relation), sat in her little accounting cage adding up figures. There was a dog that came in every day and helped himself to a tin of dog-food that he carried home in his mouth. Frank McGovern licked his pencil and wrote the price of the tin in his notebook so that Mousie Hanlon, who drove McGovern's van, could charge the owner later on when he delivered the messages to the house.

Dad always supervised the purchase of new shoes at Connolly's Shoe Shop where the young male shop assistants whipped the shoelaces back and forth like greased lightning. He always insisted on buying Clark's brown leather laced shoes for us. "Oul' rubbish," he said of the strappy ones with the heels that I adored. I knew he considered good shoes akin to good breeding or a good fire, and that my dreams of fashion were doomed for many years to come.

Chapter Eighteen

Mammy was home with us all day so we took no notice of her feeble attempts at discipline. She talked all the time, so we only listened to her with half an ear. She was always singing the praises of our cousins, Betty, Helen, and Pat, who were obliging and well-behaved. "All Aunt Nancy has to say is "Betty, set the table; Helen, sweep the floor; Pat, wash the dishes; and they do it," she marveled. But no amount of nagging or scolding could make us reform. Mammy was a softie and we knew it.

We were a little afraid of Dad. He was thin, strong, and serious-looking with his dark hair and shaggy eyebrows and that steely glint in his blue eyes. He could be great gas when he was in a good mood, but he was always reminding us that he was the master of the house and his rule was law. If he issued a command to come in from the street for tea, we jumped to do his bidding, knowing we'd get a good slap on the back of the legs if we kept him waiting. Dad's hands were big and hard. They absorbed thorns and bruises as he hammered, painted, wallpapered, pruned, and polished. His hands could fix everything from a sewer pipe to a doll's broken arm. On Saturday afternoons, when he was done with other people's gardens, Dad worked in his own garden or on a thousand other tasks around our house. "Do a job right or don't do it at all. A job worth doing is worth doing well," he told us. "Never turn back once you've put your hand to the plough." Dad was devoted to the gods of the hearth. On Sundays, he banked the fire with slack before we went out for our afternoon walk. And when we returned, cold and famished, he raked the coals into a hot flame and put the kettle on for tea.

If we wanted Dad's permission to stay out late or do something special, we went to Mammy first. "You leave it with me," she said. "I have my ways of getting around him." When it came to favors, we knew you had to go in by the tradesman's entrance and not march up to the front door as if you were Somebody. Enlisting Mammy's help with Dad was like praying to Our Lady or your patron saint to have a word with God on your behalf. We also knew that women were religious and their job was to make sure their husbands and children attended Mass and behaved like decent Catholics. Good-living, respectable husbands and fathers like Dad went to Mass and confession to please their wives, but their hearts weren't in it. A man who showed signs of being too religious was a bit of a "Holy Joe" some women might admire, but men couldn't stand the likes of him at all.

Although I loved Dad, I had to admit he could be moody and unpredictable at times. He came home from work at six o'clock most evenings and we heard him wheeling his big heavy bicycle through the archway and lifting the latch on the back door. The cat stiffened, trying to decide whether to stay curled in the big chair by the fire or flee in fear for its life. Dad did not care for cats. As he entered the kitchen, the cat jumped to the windowsill to claw at the frame for escape. Mammy ran around, throwing coal on the fire, scrubbing potatoes at the sink, and putting a saucepan of water to boil on the gas-stove. "Are you only putting the potatoes on now?" he would say as he walked into the livingroom where we all sat, doing our homework. "Isn't that a very poor fire for a man coming home from a hard day's work?" He took off his cap, picked up the poker and began to stir the coals in the fireplace. A poor fire or weak tea showed meanness of spirit, he always said. Mammy had warned us not to bother him as soon as he came in the door from work. She said he'd be tired after a long day but we knew she was waiting, like us, to see what kind of mood he was in. If he was in a good mood, he might tell us a story while we sat around the table and begged bits of dinner from his plate. If he was in a bad mood and we were listening to pop music on the radio, he'd tell us to turn off that damn noise and give him a bit of peace and quiet.

Chapter Nineteen

Sometimes Dad complained bitterly about his job at IMCO. The owner of the company was a Jew named Louis Spiro, although from the tone of Dad's anti-Semitic remarks, he might as well have been a Nazi named Adolf Eichman.

At one time there were four hundred people working at the IMCO plant and eight delivery vans operating around the city. The Hoffman Presser was the primary machine in use and the clothes were treated with percoethylene. The lads who worked in the plant would have to be taken out periodically, sat in the sun, and given a drink of milk to revive them from the fumes. "Duck's Back Cleaning" was a specialty, supposed to make the garments waterproof. "Sure it's only oul' codology," Dad said. "They all go into the same machine."

Still, working at IMCO was better than working for a brewery as Dad did for five years. He used to deliver beer to the old Jury's Hotel on Kildare Street in Dublin. "I once saw two barrows full of dead rats being taken away from the cellars," he said. "It was a kind of catacomb under the building where they kept the drink. And all this while the gentry were upstairs dining in the lap of luxury!"

Some days Dad came home in a cheerful mood. He got to know Dublin like the back of his hand and he was proud of his knowledge. He often told us what the women who ran the open-air markets on Moore Street had said to him and what he had said back. "If you happen to bump into one of their barrows, they'll skin you alive," he said. "But if you apologize and treat them with respect, they can't do enough for you." Dad prided himself on his refinement and courtesy and he didn't hesitate to paint a picture of himself as a kind of working-class saint, in comparison to the rude and selfish louts he was obliged to associate with in his everyday life.

When he wasn't lecturing us about the selfishness of other people, Dad could be very entertaining. Every night he brought home a pocketful of words for our diversion. I loved the City's strange place-names—Dolphin's Barn, Stoneybatter, Ringsend, Ballyfermot, Winetavern Street, and Chapelizod, named after the Chapel of Iseult in *King Arthur and the Knights of the Round Table*. I knew the story of Tristan and Iseult, the lovers who fled from King Mark of Cornwall across the sea to Ireland. I also knew that Uncle Christy was a quartermaster on a ship called the *Isolde*, another variation of the name.

"The only part of Dublin I hated going to was the Coombe," Dad said. "There was a terrible smell from the glue factory and you couldn't get away from it no matter where you went." The glue factory was the end of the line for workhorses like the ones that pulled the slopman's and the ragman's carts on their periodic visits to Pearse Close. Such miserable creatures were typically sent to the rendering plant or knackers' yard when they had outlived their usefulness.

Further afield from Dublin were other places with fascinating names: Leopardstown, Foxrock and Ticknock, Cawbawn Lane, and The Hellfire Club in The Devil's Glen where Mammy said the Devil used to appear at poker games. That had happened in the old days when the well-heeled toffs rode out in coaches and carriages to the Dublin Mountains in search of immoral entertainment. The Hellfire Club was a well-known venue for vice and corruption. One night, after the usual poker players arrived and were seated around the table, a tall stranger appeared among them. Nobody thought anything of it until one fellow looked under the table and saw the stranger's cloven hoof. Then the jig was up and the whole thing ended in a fiery blaze with coaches flying off into the bogs and ditches, departing in a frenzy of fear and remorse.

Chapter Twenty

Dad made it clear that our behavior reflected on his good name and he warned us never to do anything that would besmirch his reputation. You could tell a lot about people by the way they behaved and how they took care of their belongings. For instance, Dad was the only person who picked up the rubbish that other people threw around Pearse Close, and he made us do the same. He took care of his house even though it was only rented from the Corporation, and he tended his garden instead of leaving it full of weeds as many neighbors did. Mrs. Finnie, who lived opposite us, had a nice front garden with red geraniums planted next to the front door, but Dad thought it was disgraceful for a woman to have to do that kind of work. "Andy Finnie ought to be ashamed of himself," he said, "to let his poor wife do the gardening and the wall-papering. What kind of a man is he at all?"

Dad always paid cash for big items and refused to buy anything on "hire purchase." "You don't want to be like those people who live in big houses and they without the price of their breakfast!" he said. Although English television was available at the time, Dad refused to buy us a television set until Ireland had its own national station. "I will not have the Queen and her Corgis waving goodnight in my living room," he declared. Uncle Christy worked for an English company, The Irish Lights, that manned the lighthouses around the coast, and he and Aunt Nancy had had a television for years. But we had to wait until 1965 when Radio Telefis Eireann, or RTE, was established before Dad finally broke down and bought a set. He made sure to tell us that he had paid for it in cash. We had no idea how lucky we were. By the time we got television, I was twelve and already hooked on books and stories.

Dad particularly detested Friday nights when the various money collectors came to our door. It was always dark and often rainy, and the men were uniformly dressed in drab clothes, so my overall impression of them was of something elemental like a mountain or an oak tree appearing suddenly on our doorstep. The Rent Man came to collect his fifteen shillings a week for Dun Laoghaire Corporation. Sean Deegan, otherwise known as "The Insurance Man" because he worked for the New Ireland Insurance Company, came for his contribution. Willie Clifford, known as "The Other Insurance Man" or "The Penny-A-Week Man," also came on Fridays. He carried a brown leather satchel like the ones we brought to school. Dad hated him in particular. He had gone to school with Mammy, and Dad suspected he was still sweet on her. One rainy Friday night, Dad had just come in from work when there was a knock on the door. "Is that one of those Shylocks that would take the bread out of the mouths of decent working-class people?" he said loudly. "Jim, Jim," Mammy shushed him, mortified. "You know it's only Willie Clifford from Glasthule." I looked up from where I was reading my book by the fire to gauge the tension in the room. Dad might be only teasing Mammy or he might be feeling cranky and decide to go out and give Mr. Clifford a piece of his mind. Mammy grabbed her handbag and closed the livingroom door behind her so poor Mr. Clifford wouldn't hear Dad giving out. Mammy kept all the family accounts in her big black handbag and if it went astray for more than a few minutes, she got into a terrible tizzy. Dad subsided, giving me a grin to let me know he had only been taking a rise out of her.

Every so often the slopman came to Pearse Close with his horse and cart to collect our food scraps. Everything about him—his clothes, his horse and the cart—were dark brown in color. I was mad about horses and insisted on petting the slopman's horse despite the odor of decaying vegetable matter that hung perpetually around him. The eggman came during the week in his red van and sometimes brought a turkey egg for our John.

After putting in a full week as a van-driver, Dad spent his Saturday mornings gardening for two ladies, Miss Coakley and Mrs.

Moyles, who lived in Rosmeen Park, Dun Laoghaire. I loved to ride with him on the crossbar of his bike down the tree-shaded Noggin Hill, past the People's Park with its regimental flowerbeds, the rows of flowers all evenly spaced like the houses in which we lived, and the uniformed park-keeper who moodily prodded bits of rubbish with his pointed stick.

The big houses, surrounded by landscaped lawns, seemed to doze on those warm Saturdays. There was a greengage tree, a sundial, and a striped cotton door-blind, faded by sunlight. It was always sunny there and the birds sang unceasingly—it seemed another country from the one I knew in Sallynoggin. The ladies were usually out but they left a plate of biscuits for Dad. I ate the biscuits while he planted, weeded, and watered the gardens. I loved to walk through the rooms with their thick carpets, touching the curtains, fingering the fine linens, trying out chairs and sofas, imagining a life that belonged to someone else. "Don't be wishing your life away," Mammy warned me. Later I would learn that although I could keep a cool head in emergencies, the gift of living in the moment would continue to elude me.

We never had a dog of our own, but we did have a pure white, longhaired, pedigreed Persian cat to whom we gave the ignominious name of "Fluffy." Dad hated cats because they killed the birds, dug up his garden, and occupied his armchair. But Fluffy was a gift from Mrs. Moyles and she was not to be denied. "James," she said grandly when she dropped off the kitten at our house, "whatever would we do without you?"

My burgeoning awareness of class difference was further reinforced when Dad was laid up with a slipped disk and Mammy had to go out to work. She got a job as a housekeeper for the Brindleys, a well-off family in Dun Laoghaire. I walked to the Brindleys' house after school to wait for Mammy to finish her work. It was a lovely house with a manicured front garden and sweeping driveway. The Brindley girls were about the same age as my sisters and I, and I was mortified that my mother had to look after these other girls instead of her own family. The girls attended Holy Child Convent School, and I deeply resented inheriting their dark-green school uniforms and the other clothes that Mammy gratefully accepted. On the other hand, I loved snooping around the Brindleys' beautiful home, touching the furniture and imagining what it would be like to live there. My favorite place was the window seat where you could draw the long green velvet drapes and be completely hidden from view. There was nowhere like that in our house. The only room that had a lock on the door was our bathroom, and Dad was always banging on the door to make you come out so he could go in and read *The Meath Chronicle*.

Chapter Twenty-One

Although Ireland in the late 1950s and early '60s was primarily poor and we were no better off than other working-class people, Dad liked to think we were a cut above the rest. This elevated status seemed to hinge on the fact that we read books, listened to music, and didn't raise our voices—except for Dad when he was in bad humor. "It's all in the breeding," he told us, as if we had been genetically selected for a more refined way of life.

Our status also seemed to hinge on the way we spoke. Dad had a good ear for language and he prided himself on his ability to tell which of Ireland's thirty-two counties a person came from within minutes of meeting him. "So you're a Wicklow-woman?" he'd say, or "You're a Limerick man yourself, I suppose?" He was never wrong. But he hated the local accent of our neighborhood and was always telling us to "speak nicely" like educated people. We saw no difference between ourselves and our neighbors, but Dad was always reminding us that our behavior reflected on his good name and reputation. For someone who didn't seem to like the neighbors, he worried a lot about what they thought of him and of us, his children.

It was true that our parents were different from the parents of other kids on our street. For one thing, neither of them drank nor put money on dogs or horses. And Dad only swore when he hit his finger with a hammer or when he thought there were no women present. Moreover, Mammy read voraciously, Dad played Irish music on the fiddle, and their favorite outing was to the Gas Company Theatre in Dun Laoghaire to see all the popular Irish plays. You went in through the big glass doors of the Company showroom and made your way through the rows of gleaming cookers and gas geysers to the stairs that led up to the tiny theatre. The plays filled Dad with national pride and he would tell us, with tears in his eyes, about Joxer Daly and Pegeen Mike, *The Shadow of a Gunman* and *Riders to the Sea*. He'd strike a pose in the kitchen doorway and raise a hand to his brow as if gazing into the middle distance. "I often used to ask meself," he'd say in a thick Dublin accent, "what is the stars?" Though he liked imitating the actors, Dad always insisted that they spoke with the tongues of angels in their everyday lives.

He admired the cultivated accents of the newsreaders on RTE, the new Irish TV station, and the way that other educated, professional people spoke. He also insisted that doctors, dentists, and politicians should be referred to by their proper titles. It was our President, *Mister* Eamon DeValera, and not "oul Dev," as the locals referred to him. Our Taoiseach, the Prime Minister, deserved to be called *Mister* Sean Lemass. *Doctor* Russell and *Mister* Brown, the chemist, were educated men who deserved our respect. We thought this was the height of nonsense, particularly in the case of Doctor Russell, who shouted at us when Mammy was sick. He came to our house with his black bag under his arm and his face like thunder.

"Come here till I murther yis, yis dirty little Arabs," a mother from Sallynoggin might call to her children in those politically incorrect times. "I'll swing for that lad one of these days, Missus," a neighbor would say, shaking her head. "You'll never rear that child, Missus," a woman once observed to my mother after examining our twins in their pram and noting the difference in their sizes. "That little wan isn't long for this world." People loved to tease one another about age and decrepitude. "That fella's so old you can smell the clay off him," they'd say cheerfully. "Didn't he go off very fast in the end all the same?" they'd remark when someone died. "Ah, isn't he better off out of it, Missus?" was the usual response. "Isn't he in a better place now?" "Amn't I the right eejit," a younglad would ask rhetorically, "I'm after forgettin' me bike!" "Yis are after takin' me favorite conker," one kid would accuse another after losing his prize chestnut. "Gizzit back!"

As a family, we had always taken pleasure in wordplay. We listened to "The Maureen Potter Show" every Sunday afternoon on the radio and laughed with delight at all the Dublin accents Maureen and her partner Jimmy O'Dea could imitate. It was all very well to listen to the radio, even to do our own imitations, but Dad made it clear that he didn't want us talking like that in public.

Chapter Twenty-Two

By the age of thirteen, I had reached the end of my primary education at St. Joseph's School on Tivoli Road, Dun Laoghaire. The nuns must have mistaken my good behavior for intellectual promise because they arranged for me to receive free tuition to attend Saint Joseph of Cluny Secondary School for Girls, a private Catholic school in Killiney. It was 1965 and a new government scheme was about to provide free secondary education in Ireland for the first time. Cluny, however, had opted out of the new scheme and remained a private, fee-paying school. Dad was delighted at the honor I'd received, even though it meant that I would have to have an expensive uniform and money for books and supplies.

The first task was to tog me out in the required uniform, so Mammy took me to Arnott's on Grafton Street in Dublin to be fitted for whatever this might entail. The uniform turned out to be an elaborate affair with a Royal blue pleated gymslip, yellow blouse and blue dickey-bow for summer, as well as a blue blazer and hat that sported the Cluny badge. For winter, there was an orange sweater, fastened with the ubiquitous dickey-bow, as well as an overcoat, gloves, and special indoor and outdoor shoes. Also required was a knee-length divided-skirt, Aertex blouse, and plimsole shoes for gym class, as well as black runners and a hockey stick for sports. Like the fictional Malory Towers ("I say, Darrell, jolly hockeysticks and all that"), Cluny espoused English games like hockey rather than camogie, the Irish version of hurling for women. Poor Mammy was delighted to discover that secondhand uniforms were available at a reduced price. We combed through the faded gymslips and oversized blazers. "She'll grow into them, Missus," the shop assistant assured her. Mammy had never understood my mortification at having to wear secondhand clothes and was only too grateful whenever her old friend Mags O'Reilly brought a bag of cast-off clothes from her daughter Mary who was my own age.

"You'll be a real snob now," Aunt Nancy said when she heard I had been accepted at Cluny. "We won't be good enough for you." Aunt Nancy was fond of Dad but she had no patience with his social climbing aspirations. Our cousins Betty and Helen, and the other girls from their neighborhood, planned to attend the free secondary school at Haddington Road in Dublin. They would all ride the bus together every morning and evening, whereas I would have to ride my bicycle alone over the fields behind the church to Killiney.

As soon as Dad heard that elocution classes were offered on Saturday mornings at St. Joseph of Cluny, nothing would do him but to have me sign up. He had seen and admired the elocution teacher, Miss Margaret O'Brien, when she appeared on RTE. Miss O'Brien was one of several continuity announcers in the mid-1960s who told the viewers which channel they were watching, what they were about to see in the next program, and who had presented and produced the previous one. Most important of all, continuity announcers played music during programming intervals and filled in if there were service breakdowns. There were long gaps between programs in the early days of RTE and, apart from the continuity announcers, the only diversion was a static picture of a Saint Brigid's Cross on the screen for hours on end. Miss O'Brien wore a long dress and played the harp on television and Dad thought her the very image of lovely Irish womanhood, a modern Maud Gonne MacBride or Caitlin Ní Houlihan made flesh. His fond hope was that I would one day become a continuity announcer too. The only thing I wanted was to please Dad, so I dutifully agreed to attend elocution class.

Miss O'Brien held court at a long table in the big empty Assembly Hall where the whole school met every morning before class. I was awed by her glamorous appearance. She wore perfume and flawless make-up, and her hair always looked as if it had just been set by a hairdresser. By the time I had ridden to school on my bicycle in the rain, the pleats had fallen out of my secondhand gymslip and I felt like the epitome of a grubby schoolgirl. We studied labials and bilabials, diphthongs and dentals, vowels and consonants. I liked to watch Miss O'Brien's lipsticked mouth open wide as she recited "AY as in *gay*, *EE* as in *eel*, *I* as *eye*, *O* as in *old*, *OO* as in *glue*." Most fascinating of all were her long manicured fingernails which caused her to scrabble helplessly on the table when she tried to pick up a pen or pencil. How did she ever make a cup of tea for herself, I wondered, or avoid getting ladders in her nylons with nails like those?

Although I was aware of class differences, it wasn't until I attended Cluny that I began to be ashamed of my home and family and to be conscious of my working-class accent. Elocution made me even more aware of my shortcomings and the differences between my family and the families of those better-off girls who were my fellow students. Like all working-class Irish children, my brother, sisters and I had always called our mother "Mammy." "I'm straight telling my Mammy on you," was an oft-repeated if somewhat empty threat on our street. I noticed that my friends at Cluny called their mothers "Mum" or even "Mummy." Then there was the fact that my father rode a bicycle to work while one of my classmates was dropped off at school in a Mercedes. We lived in a rented house that had its door and window-frames painted every other year by Dun Laoghaire Corporation, whereas other girls lived in private houses with their own names – "Knocknagow" and "Rinn Na Mara"- emblazoned on the front gates.

Other girls' mothers were always plying me with food, and I spent a lot of time at their family dinner tables, picking up hints on table manners. I began to notice some horrifying lapses in my own family. Dad always had potatoes with his dinner, and he had a habit of mashing the potatoes together with the rest of his food and eating off his knife instead of his fork. And why had I never noticed the sounds he made when he drank his tea? If the tea was too hot, he poured a little into his saucer and tipped it up to his mouth to drink.

I cringed inwardly.

For elocution class I had to memorize and recite a series of sentimental poems like "Tim the Irish Terrier" and "All in an April Evening," making sure to open my mouth wide and pronounce each syllable as I spoke. Later at home I recited the poems to Dad and he noted with approval my refined accent and ladylike demeanor.

Our Mary, who was two years younger than I and far more brazen, attended the local technical school. Her response to Dad's admonitions to speak nicely and stand up straight was to hike up her skirt, stick out her considerable chest, and speak in the flattest Sallynoggin accent she could muster. Dad winced but there was nothing he could do to make her behave.

Before I began to use my bike to get to school, I walked there with another girl from Sallynoggin. Marie had long hair with a fringe that fell straight down into her eyes. Fringes were strongly discouraged by the nuns who inspected our uniforms and general appearance on a daily basis. Marie also wore black mascara, the kind that came in a little box with a brush you spit on before rubbing it on the block of paint and applying it in thick clumps to your lashes. She was what the nuns called "common," definitely not Cluny material. I was too concerned with fitting in and emulating the appearance (and especially the table manners) of my fellow students to appreciate Marie's refusal to be cowed by other people's opinions. In the first of many experiences of moral cowardice, I felt relieved when she dropped out of school and I no longer had to walk with her every morning.

I made friends with several girls from the adjoining neighborhoods of Killiney and Glenageary, and I spent a good deal of time at their houses. I never invited them to mine, partly out of embarrassment at my lowly circumstances but also because there was no privacy at home. I shared a room with my two sisters and Dad did not welcome strangers in the house.

My sense of shame went deeper than material circumstances. I thought my body was terrifically ugly, all the more so when body hair developed but my chest remained flat as a billiard-table. My friend Kate was vain about her reddish-gold hair, which she referred to as "Titian blonde." Those were the days of long straight hair and Kate refused to swim or go out in the rain because the dampness made her hair curly. I was amazed at this preoccupation with appearances–it never occurred to me that my own self-loathing was similarly self-centered—and I envied Kate's vanity. It was hard to imagine her mother ever fine-combing Kate's hair and applying "Sulio." I began letting my hair grow as soon as I started secondary school and had the satisfaction of producing a mane of thick, fashionably straight hair that I was sure Kate envied, though she would never admit it.

My sisters and I spent hours washing each other's hair with concoctions of rosemary and chamomile, brewed according to Mammy's instructions. She told us about the benefits of slathering our faces with egg-whites and buttermilk, putting slices of cucumber on our eye-lids and washing our hands with porridge-oats. Our eternal grooming drove Dad crazy. He was forever banging on the bathroom door, newspaper in hand, asking why in God's name we were always washing. From time to time he had to take the pipes apart to remove what looked like a bird's nest of hair. "The three witches," he called us, shaking his head in disgust at our long sheets of hair as we sat around the dinner table.

Dad loved to rail about Socialism. "The poor we have always with us," he would intone bitterly. Mammy worried out loud about how hard up we were compared to some of the people she had known in her youth. Her friend Margaret O'Reilly was a case in point. She had grown up across the street from Mammy but had married "above her station." "Margaret O'Reilly," Mammy used to say, "or Maggie Smith that was. Oh, Maggie was good enough for us but not for her husband, Austin. She was always *Margaret* to him." Austin had a great job in the Post Office with a good pension that presumably gave him the right to call his wife whatever name he chose.

Chapter Twenty-Three

I always thought we were a happy, well-adjusted family until sometime around my fifteenth birthday when I seemed to switch overnight from thinking of myself as Daddy's little girl to viewing him as a cruel tyrant whose goal was to prevent me from ever having a life. The only weapons I had were stubbornness and a burning desire to discover whatever it was he and other adults were hiding from me. What did they mean when they said, "Ah, sure let them keep their innocence as long as they can"?

Mammy was always issuing advice on what I should do in any given situation, so I never learned to trust my own instincts. Instead I developed devious ways of defying her authority. I would listen to her recommendations on which girls to befriend and which to avoid and which clothes were suitable for each occasion. "Now your mother wouldn't send you out in something that didn't look nice, would she?" she'd ask rhetorically. I'd nod as if in agreement, then go and do—or wear—exactly the opposite of what she suggested. The art of passive resistance, while not the most effective or psychologically healthy response, nevertheless became my default setting. "The most stubborn girl to ever wear out shoe-leather" was how Mammy referred to me when I refused her well-meant directives.

One summer when I was about fifteen, my cousins' Auntie Betty offered to get us summer jobs at Bolands Biscuit Factory in Deansgrange where she had worked for years. Our John always had a summer job so I felt obliged to be responsible too. On the appointed day, my cousins and I showed up at the factory at eight o'clock sharp to punch the time-clock and leave our things in the locker room. We had to put on white coats and tie turbans around our heads. The factory floor was huge with different stations for the different brands.

At each station, long lines of *Marietta Biscuits, Custard Creams, Billy Bolands* and other biscuits of all shapes and sizes moved on a rolling band towards the women who waited to pack them in big square tins for the shops. I was stationed next to the *Cream Cracker* band and I tried to emulate the women who lifted entire rows of the square crackers between their two hands and fitted them deftly into the tins. Most of mine ended up in a pile that moved inexorably past me, down to the next woman on duty. At first the women indulged my mistakes, but they got fed up with the extra work and were not slow in telling me to hurry up and get a move on. It seemed hours before there was a tea-break. Everyone had to clock in and out for that too. All the women sat in the crowded locker-room, smoking cigarettes and drinking cups of tea, chatting amiably as if being chained to a factory floor all day was the most ordinary thing in the world, which of course it was. I was only there for the summer, I thought, but they were lifers. I couldn't get over it. Even the staff sale of broken biscuits on Friday nights was small consolation for my own realization—I was a working-class girl who was ill-suited to this sort of work. All I wanted to do was to go home and hide among my books where I would be safe from the real world.

I had always loved to draw and paint, although it was the names of the poster paints that chiefly delighted me. As a teenager, I fantasized about going to art school. "Now, dear," my parents said, "painting is a nice hobby, but people like us don't go to art school." Of course they were right and I had my head in the clouds as usual. But I hated that word "hobby" with its implications of meaningless busywork, something to while away the time, rather than a passion that might transform your life.

That was my problem with religion too. Didn't Jesus say "By their fruits ye shall know them"? And yet here were the adults I knew, going to Mass every Sunday, listening to sermons about the evils of self-love and the need to change one's life, then going home and not changing a thing. When I protested this hypocrisy, the answer invariably was

"Ah sure, it's only an hour on Sundays and it won't do you any harm." I was outraged. I wanted fire and passion and conviction and the lofty ideals I found in books. When Jehovah's Witnesses and Mormons came to the door, I always invited them to come in, in hopes of having an interesting conversation about religion. But it didn't take long to realize that those well-meaning missionaries had no interest in intellectual ideas. They pretended to listen but they were only indulging me. Conversion, not conversation, was all they wanted. It was deeply disappointing.

Chapter Twenty-Four

Around age fifteen or sixteen, John and I came under the influence of a young priest, Father Matt Mulvaney. He was always at odds with the local clergy but the laity loved his fiery Sunday morning sermons. I was one of a group of teenagers he gathered around him and we often visited his rooms in the Rectory. He wore a leather jacket, smoked like a chimney and had a poster of Che Guevara on the wall. It was the first time I'd heard Jesus described as a revolutionary. Father Matt organized "hops" where young people could meet and dance to music on long-playing records. On Sundays after Mass, John and I and the other teenagers in Father Matt's flock would huddle together, talking and smoking *Majors*, the strongest cigarettes on the market, until our fingers were stained yellowish-brown to the knuckles. For a while, religion actually seemed cool.

It wasn't long before my innate rebelliousness emerged, prompted as always by language. John and I joined forces over music and poetry. We read the Liverpool Beats and *The Oxford Book of Modern Verse*, and a Penguin trilogy called *Voices* that combined folk ballads with poetry and photographs. I spent long evenings in John's darkened room, listening to music and formulating vague thoughts about escaping from home and my father's watchful eye. I was no longer interested in what Mammy was reading or in Dad's approval. When I refused to go to Sunday Mass, Dad hit the ceiling. "It's all those damn books you've been reading," he fumed. When John became a first-year student at University College Dublin, I read all the books in his English literature course, including *Tess of the D'Urbervilles*, *A Passage to India* and *Eight Great Tragedies*, a collection of plays by Ibsen, Sophocles, Shakespeare, and O'Neill. These books made a huge impression on me, although I understood only a fraction of what I was reading at the time. Then I discovered J.P. Donleavy's "The Gingerman" which featured Bewley's Cafe in Dublin and the pathetic Miss Frost. As a result, my impression of sex was of something damp and dingy, closer to masturbation (although I didn't yet know the word) than to any romantic concept of love.

Armed with this smattering of education, I threw myself into arguing points of religion and philosophy with Dad. Why should I go to mass because it was only an hour on Sundays and it wouldn't do me any harm when I didn't believe in what I was saying? Why did he care about what the neighbors, the priest and his older sister Ann would think of my behavior? Why was sex before marriage "the law of the jungle" when sex after marriage was "holy matrimony"? It was shaping up to be a long and heartbreaking adolescence for both of us.

It was around this time that John began taking me to the pub with his friends. He told me what to order—a glass of Harp lager with lime—so I would not look like too much of an eejit or too conspicuously under age. Those were also the days of tennis-club dances in Sandycove and Sandymount. I was allowed to go as long as John accompanied me. The tennis clubs were dark and the music was ear-splitting. For hours I'd dance with a boy I could hardly see or hear, then walk outside with him, only to find he had spotty skin and no conversation. But the next day at school the notes passed and the whispered conversations implied that the romance of the century had just taken place.

One night when I came home late from a tennis-club dance, Dad was beside himself. He had stayed up waiting to intercept me at the top of the stairs, alarm clock in hand, as I tried to sneak into the bedroom. Next morning at breakfast he limped around the living room with his hand to the small of his back, emitting the odd groan of pain and anguish. It was obviously all my fault. At last he turned and faced the two framed pictures on our living room wall: Robert Emmet, the Irish martyr, in his high collar and velvet jacket, and Jesus holding out his Sacred Heart with its crown of thorns. Dad fell to his knees with his arms outstretched. "Is this what you died for?" he beseeched the two of them in a choking voice. I could stand it no longer. There was only one way to resolve the situation and that was for me to give in and say the magic words. "I'm sorry, Daddy," I mumbled. There was a long pause. "That's all right then," Dad muttered, getting up on his feet again. Within five minutes he had straightened up, all back pain forgotten and peace temporarily restored.

In that intergenerational combat of the late 1960s, religion was the usual battlefield. By this time Father Matt was long gone and I was questioning everything I had been taught. Other teenagers told their parents they were going to Mass but went instead to the billiard hall or met their friends to laugh and talk and smoke cigarettes. I lived in the world of ideas, so I tackled Dad head-on about religion. I passionately argued points of theology and refused to attend Mass again until I had made up my own mind about my beliefs. Every Sunday morning heralded a showdown with Dad. "You'd better be gone to the church when we come home," he told me as he and Mammy left the house for an early service. When he returned and found me still there, stubborn and unrepentant, he was furious. "As long as you live in my house, you'll keep my rules and do what I say," he thundered. But short of throwing me out on the street, there was not much he could do to make me behave.

I knew that my bravado was just a show of force. I was still clueless about sex. Whenever I was alone with a boy and he tried to place my hand on the bulge in his trousers, I had no idea what to do. I knew I was supposed to attract men, but I also understood that I was supposed to keep them at bay. What was that bulge all about anyway? It would be several decades before I discovered my own sexuality in all its joyful unruliness. As for religion, I was toiling up the Noggin Hill towards home one day when I was struck, like Paul on the road to Damascus, with an acute sense of loss. There was no god out there, no guardian angel, no patron saint. I was all alone in the universe and it was a terrifying prospect. I thrust the fear aside but it was to return later on in America after I left my husband. I was alone in a vast continent with no one belonging to me, no one whose job it was to take care of me. It would be many years before I realized that growing up entailed assuming that responsibility myself.

Conflicts with Dad escalated as we children grew older. During the "Summer of Love" in 1968, my sisters and I made peace with each other and became the best of friends, presenting a united front against Dad's authoritarian rule. His problem was that he loved us and didn't know how to let us go. He had no concept of independence, and he saw no reason why his daughters should ever leave home except to get married. "Do we beat you? Do we starve you?" he asked when I was nineteen and beginning to make noises about getting a place of my own. He made it hard to leave but also necessary. The flower-children of the Sixties with their notions of individualism and free-thinking were completely alien to him. I aspired to joining the hippies who seemed to be voicing all the frustration I was unable to express. I saw Dad as the gatekeeper who stood between me and my quest for Love and Romance.

Chapter Twenty-Five

In 1969 when I somehow managed to pass the Leaving Certificate and graduate from secondary school, I had no idea what to do next. I had no discernible skills except the gift of memorization which I had used to fix all of Bob Dylan's lyrics in my long-term memory. I had a burning desire to leave home in search of adventure, but no way of supporting myself in the real world. Into this uncertainty, Dad pressed me to go to secretarial school where I might at least learn something useful. It was a humiliating choice after my fantasies of art college and excitement, but I complied when I discovered other school chums who were doing the same thing. Secretarial classes took place in the basement of a house on Merrion Road. They were led by two elderly spinster ladies who wore their hair in buns and strongly resembled the Daughters of the Heart of Mary nuns of my childhood. I was an indifferent student and later an abysmal secretary. My heart just wasn't in it, although I loved playing the part of "young woman about town." I took up smoking in earnest which made me feel mature and sophisticated but, given my taste for affectation and excess, I went a step further. In a tiny tobacconist shop on Baggot Street, I discovered smelly Gauloise cigarettes, which sported the winged helmet of the ancient Gauls on the packet and were favored by Jean-Paul Sartre and Pablo Picasso. I was likewise charmed by the black paper and gold foil filter tips of Sobranie Black Russian cigarettes, which I smoked on the top deck of the double-decker bus as it careened home to Sallynoggin after work. It was a good thing that I learned to type, not only because I eventually became a writer, but also because it enabled me to get a job at the University of Vermont and embark on a belated college career.

Years later when I went home to visit Dad, who was living alone by then, I offered to read him some of my work. He had always loved my voice and he listened raptly to the poems and stories I had composed. When I was done, he gazed at me in admiration. "Do you mean to tell me," he said in tones of awe, "that you typed all that yourself?"

Looking back at that tumultuous time, I can see that Dad and I were on different sides of an enormous cultural divide. His traditional Irish Catholic, working-class concept of what was normal, proper and expected, and my infatuation with everything American and new and unconventional, made it impossible for us to understand each other. It wasn't just the books I read or the folk music I adored or the fairly innocent drugs I sampled—fat joints of tobacco and crumbled hashish, magic mushrooms, a few tabs of acid—it was the sense that the world was out there passing me by and I was desperate to be part of it. In other words, I was a classic teenager, full of affectations and desires without the slightest idea of how to achieve them. I could not understand how my parents could be content with a life that did not include change or serendipity. All they wanted was peace and quiet and respectability, children they could crow about a little but not too much, and a bit of comfort and security in their old age. I still cringe when I consider my own naiveté, my scathing criticism of all they held dear, and my absolute conviction of so much I did not understand.

If Dad suspected that my noble declarations represented nothing more than the desire to ruin my life by having sex outside the bonds of Holy Matrimony, he wasn't far off. He was disgusted when I eventually moved out of the house to a tiny bed-sitter by the seafront in Dun Laoghaire. After nosing out the local hippie enclave in Dun Laoghaire, I had met a young American draft-dodger who epitomized everything my family was not. He was a long-haired, bearded hippie but his mother was a bluestocking from New England and his father was an English professor and a poet. My escape from Sallynoggin was underway.

Looking back now through the long telescope of years, I can see how many small willful acts—they could hardly have been called decisions—influenced my life in ways I could not have foreseen at the time. When I moved out of the house against my father's wishes, I had no idea that I was in the process of losing not just my accent but my culture along with it. I would spend the next few decades trying in vain to retrieve the latter and explain the absence of the former.

Chapter Twenty-Six

Until 1979, Irish law acknowledged that owning and using contraceptive devices and pills was legal, but they could not be imported or sold in Ireland. There were loopholes, of course, like the family planning clinics that would offer contraceptives to married women in exchange for a donation, but such clinics were few and far between. Unmarried women and girls were generally out of luck. It wasn't until 1985 that the Irish government finally defied the Catholic Church and approved the sale of contraceptives.

I don't know what it would have been like to have had a decent sex education and access to contraception. Mammy had always said that she and Dad thanked God for the children they were given and she felt sorry for the young women nowadays with so many decisions to make. I had never imagined getting married and having children when I grew up and, being shy and bookish, I had generally avoided babies and small children as much as possible. But my American boyfriend and I played a hit or miss game with sex and fertility and I got pregnant when I was twenty and he was twenty-four. His aunt and uncle, with whom he had been living since coming to Ireland, embraced us and took us under their ample wing. We married shortly thereafter, further infuriating Dad and breaking Mammy's heart by refusing to get married in the Catholic Church.

The early 1970s saw the beginning of The Irish Women's Movement in which several female firebrands drew attention to the dismal situation of women in Ireland. At that time, Irish women workers earned only 55 percent of men's wages so that most women left their jobs when they married. And marriage automatically barred women from working in the Civil Service. But I was preoccupied with my own life and took little interest in political issues. I had, of course, quit my loathsome secretarial job when I married and I threw myself into my new role as wife and expectant mother. I loved the novelty of being pregnant and the new sense of direction it gave me. We rented a damp basement flat in Monkstown with a long hallway and rooms that were impossible to heat. Money was scarce since my husband, as a foreigner and a draft-dodger, could not legally work in Ireland. But there were plenty of pick-up jobs among the hippies who painted and papered and did construction work, in addition to making leather sandals and handbags and sometimes selling hashish.

My son was born in Holles Street Hospital in September and his Irish grandfather was glad to embrace him now that I was actually a respectable married woman. His American grandfather was thrilled that his grandson had been born in the very "lying-in" hospital that Joyce had made famous in *Ulysses*. I was born here too, I thought, but my history had become irrelevant. Nevertheless, I became a devoted mother, amazed to find myself so connected, body and soul, to another human being. My husband was equally devoted and he did his share of walking the floor of our basement flat with the screaming baby, changing nappies, and reading baby instruction books, though none seemed to have the kind of answers we needed in the moment.

Motherhood straightened me up in many ways, not least of which was my attitude to food. Heavily influenced by my new American relatives, I embraced the "back to nature" craze of the early Seventies and became a born-again earth-mother who cooked everything from scratch and was a devout proponent of breastfeeding. But in Ireland my "notions" frequently earned more ridicule than regard. I remember sitting in the waiting room of the Patrick Street Dispensary in Dun Laoghaire with my son, who was about six months old at the time. We were waiting for one of the usual check-ups or the vaccinations that all young mothers dread. Seated next to me was a buxom, older woman with a fat, jowly infant on her lap. We exchanged the usual formalities about our babies – their genders, names and ages. Her baby, who was busily sucking on a bottle, was twice the size of mine, although, as it turned out, exactly the same age. I felt defeated with my long hair and hippie clothes, my baby clutched in a blue *Mothercare* sling. I had nothing to defend myself with except a head full of Freudian psychoanalysis and Adele Davis's dubious American nutritional theories. When the other woman discovered I was persisting with breastfeeding, she didn't hesitate to tell me what she thought. "Sure, a little slip of a thing like you couldn't feed a baby," she said loudly. "Give the poor *craythur* a bottle, for God's sake!"

My knowledge of Freudian psychoanalysis had come from my association with The Irish Psycho-Analytic Association, formed in Dublin in 1942 by a charismatic Englishman who practiced and taught an unorthodox, radical Christian approach to psychoanalysis. My American relatives were deeply involved in the group and its bohemian ethos also attracted those of us hippies who sought intellectual stimulation and, for some, a cure for what ailed us.

What had ailed me for most of my life was a kind of low-level melancholy. Perhaps it was moodiness, or willfulness, or the acute self-consciousness I felt around other people. It seemed a natural thing to turn to one of the psychoanalysts for help. The one I chose was a handsome older man who bore a discomfiting resemblance to my father. His room was dark and softly lit with a long couch in the corner. After a few awkward sessions in which no one said anything very much that I recall, he came over and sat beside me on the couch. What was this? I had come to him for guidance, but all he did was sit there, murmuring sympathetically and fondling my breasts, while I tried to think of a polite excuse to get him to stop. I was an awful *gawm* in those days.

Chapter Twenty-Seven

Several years later found us living in yet another basement flat in Dun Laoghaire. It was a big place with a backyard and nearby woods, but the bathroom was freezing cold and my husband and son both suffered from asthma because of the damp. It seemed serendipitous when President Carter granted amnesty to Vietnam-era draft resisters and we began talking of emigrating to America.

"Sure there's no future for the young people in Ireland," Mammy said in her annoyingly cheerful way, "and it's dear-earned butter that's licked off a briar." But my father was heartbroken. "What's the point of making money when it's not your own land, your own country?" he said mournfully, echoing generations of poverty-stricken Irish people. It was a warm summer that year. The gardens seemed lovelier than ever as we visited our friends and distributed all the things we would not be taking with us—breadboards and chopping-blocks, pots and pans, an entire coffee service we'd been given as a wedding present. In between, I tried to cheer up Dad by telling him we'd surely be home in six months or a year. "I'll try it for a little while," I said, ever the one to put my head in the sand.

We arrived in Milton, Vermont, in October 1977. I wore a long skirt, had hair down to my waist, and I hid my shyness under a cloud of cigarette smoke. On the main street of Milton, we shared a large apartment with my brother-in-law in a dilapidated old mansion that had once been occupied by the village doctor. There were squirrels, chipmunks, and bluejays everywhere. On those first autumn mornings the kitchen was full of sunshine and the house smelled of rich, seasoned wood. But I refused to be charmed. I was baffled by my husband's delight in our new surroundings and by my little boy's newfound American accent. All of a sudden, I was supposed to answer to "Mom" and I hardly recognized myself in the title. My Irish accent was a terrible embarrassment to my son and I sometimes found myself at the center of a group of giggling four-year-olds who thought my use of "trolley" instead of "shopping-cart" and "trousers" instead of "pants" was utterly hilarious. The last straw was the nice, middle-class neighbor who telephoned to invite me to her house across the street. I wasn't used to the telephone and couldn't understand why she didn't simply knock at the back door and come in like a normal person.

Winter came, bringing with it more snow than I had ever imagined. Cars got stuck in the parking-lot. The sound of spinning wheels and throbbing engines could be heard at all hours. My son, togged out in a snowmobile suit and insulated boots, dug tunnels for his toy cars and made igloos in the backyard. My dreams were full of images of home—a Dublin street-corner, seagulls wheeling across the bay, fog climbing over a garden wall—and all were more vivid than the bright day beginning outside. The narrowness of Irish life seemed suddenly filled with warmth and security; friends and family were precious and irreplaceable. A letter from home could trigger days of misery and I wallowed in homesickness and self-pity. What was the matter with me, I wondered. Americans moved all the time. They went away to college, followed their jobs all over the country, bade farewell to friends and relatives, apparently with few regrets. But I had no experience of running my own life or making decisions about my future. All I knew how to do was rebel against authority and then founder in the emptiness it left behind.

During my first spring in Vermont, I signed up for driving lessons with the local high school instructor and discovered the true meaning of terror. Mammy, fresh off the boat for a long visit, couldn't understand my dread of being in the driver's seat. But then again, neither she nor my sisters had ever learned to drive. In fact, no one I knew had had a car when I was a child. Dad drove a van for a living but he rode a bicycle to work. Here I was, driving on the wrong side of the road, my knuckles turning white on the steering-wheel while

Mammy and my son sang the "clutch-and-brake" song to encourage me from the back seat. I had no intention of staying longer than six months in America, although I had equally no idea of where I would go at the end of that time. I did manage to get a driver's license but that was no solution for my fears. With no concept of independence and no path towards achieving it, I was well and truly stuck in the Frozen North.

Chapter Twenty-Eight

We didn't stay long in Milton. After a year or so, we bought an old house in Winooski and formed a family-style communal household with my brother-in-law and a beloved cousin. I continued to keep house while casting about for solutions to my depression. There were numerous mental health practitioners but none seemed able to bridge the cultural divide I felt so keenly, and most contented themselves with predictable clichés that made me long for psychoanalysis, which at least had depth, notwithstanding its other shortcomings. When my son was about eight years old, I applied for a secretarial job at the University of Vermont. Despite my acute shyness and woeful typing skills, I got the job, which provided a salary as well as health and dental benefits for my family. I was on my way to work there when the man with the gun stepped into my life.

When I looked out of the car window, all I could see was my own terrified reflection. It was getting dark outside and I had no idea where we were. "Just let me go," I said. "Just let me out here, okay?" That made him mad. "Stop saying that," he said, "or you'll be sorry." I thought about my apartment in an old house by the Winooski River Falls and wished I was there, studying for my exam over a glass of wine. My son hated the place and I didn't blame him. It was large, empty, and cold. At age eleven, he was convinced I had ruined his life and I was afraid it was true. When I had left our old house, I had taken almost nothing except my clothes and a few of my own possessions. I couldn't bear the thought that he might notice an absence in his normal environment. My own absence was another story. It was supposed to be a few months' separation from my husband, but I waited in vain for a clear signal that would let me know whether or not to return home. In the midst of my waffling, he found other substitutes and finally a permanent partner who moved in and resolved the issue. I was devastated, but as Mammy would have surely reminded me, I had no one to blame but myself.

Since leaving my husband, I'd had sex with a few men—some old friends who had taken an elder-brotherly interest in me in the past but now saw me in a new available light; some men from the office, even one who had become a regular boyfriend for a while. But I could never take them seriously, could not imagine replacing my family with one of them. And my son hated them all, particularly Mr. Regular, who was clueless about the Oedipal implications of his role as rival for an only child's perceived prerogative—his mother's attention.

I told myself I was looking for an adult relationship, but in reality, I was trying to find someone to take care of me, rescue me from this place where I had landed by mistake, take me in out of the cold Frozen North. I was like the confused baby bird that missed the experience of imprinting and asked cows, planes, and steam shovels the Big Question – "Are you my mother?" Although I was over thirty, I had never had a checkbook of my own, so I kept overpaying the gas and electric bills and the companies had to send refund checks in the mail. "I keep telling you, Angela," Mammy would have said, "cut your garment according to your cloth." But that was part of the problem—my parents had always told me what to do and now here I was, in a car with a lunatic, hurtling down the highway to God only knew where.

"Hey," the man said, "keep talking." I cast about for something to say. And so the interminable journey continued, with me describing growing up in Dublin, the city and the noisy streets full of young mothers and children, the way people talked—all that I missed which was everything I had ever known. Then he told me his story, although I knew it was probably a lie. He had broken out of jail that morning, he said, and they were searching for him all over the state. He had to steal a car so that he could get away in a hurry. He talked about the guards and the wardens and how badly they treated him. "You know about the Weathermen?" he said. "I'm one of them." That sounded a bit far-fetched, even to me. He was just a skinny little guy in jeans and an oversized plaid shirt with lank hair and a nervous manner. But maybe he was telling the truth? Either way, his life sounded even worse than mine. "I'm never going back there," he said fiercely. It is typical of who I was at the time that I began to feel sorry for him instead of furious at what he was doing to me.

By the time we crossed the state line into Massachusetts he was actually apologizing for the inconvenience. He pulled into a town close to the highway (later I discovered it was Springfield) and directed me to the bus-station among the cluster of lights off to the left. "Hand over your wallet," he said, and I reluctantly complied. He took out a five-dollar bill and gave it to me. "For the bus," he said, as he stuffed my wallet in his pocket. "But don't forget," he went on in a louder, shakier, more belligerent tone, "I have your driver's license and I know where you live. And I have friends who can find you. Don't go to the police or you'll be sorry." I had no doubt he meant what he said. I grabbed my bag of books and stumbled out of the car. As I watched the taillights disappear into the darkness, I wondered if I would ever see my old Subaru again.

Chapter Twenty-Nine

The Springfield bus-station was almost worse than the kidnapping experience. After I phoned home and arranged for someone to come and rescue me, a young black man sat down next to me and began chatting me up. Instead of moving away or telling him to leave me alone, I politely tried to ignore him by hiding in my books, although my hands were still shaking uncontrollably. The florescent lights were blinding and the station smelled of nicotine and body-odor. It would be hours before I arrived at the police station in Burlington, by which time I had made up my mind to tell all. I had to repeat my story over and over again to various disbelieving officers. Finally, one of them showed me a set of mug shots and I had no trouble picking out the man who had abducted me and stolen my car. It turned out that the same fellow had picked up a girl the day before and had raped her before she managed to get away. Suddenly I felt ill and said that I wanted to go home now. When a detective dropped me off at my dark apartment, I went inside, took off all my clothes, and stood under the rickety shower for a long time, trying and failing to wash away the whole experience.

It was bad enough that kidnapping across state lines was a federal offense so I had an FBI agent following me around for a month. More disturbing for me was the reaction of the all-female office staff at work. They demanded they be escorted to the parking lot by University security police, despite the fact that this was a unique event and highly unlikely to happen again. Since the perpetrator was long gone, I considered them all a bunch of ninnies and resolved not to let fear rule my life.

When I told my Anthropology professor that I couldn't take the exam because I had been kidnapped, he looked understandably skeptical. But the local newspaper confirmed my story. "This student is very fortunate not to have been seriously assaulted and injured in the kidnapping," the article stated. "The only reason she was not was her extraordinary level-headedness and composure during the ordeal." I knew perfectly well that I did not deserve such praise. What looked like level-headedness and composure was just resignation to ill-luck and despair over the state of my life. To make matters worse, just as I was hoping to collect the insurance money for my stolen car, the wretched thing was found in a ditch near Springfield and I had to pick it up and drive it, covered in fingerprint dust, all the way back to Burlington.

A few months later, a friend sent a newspaper clipping from *The Philadelphia Inquirer*. Apparently, my abductor was wanted for murdering a nurse and stuffing her body in the trunk of a car. Meanwhile police "up and down the East Coast" were re-examining old murder cases to see if the man could be a suspect. Among those old cases was the January 1975 stabbing death of a 17-year-old high school senior in the parking lot of the Oxford Valley Mall in Bucks County, Pennsylvania. My kidnapper's name was listed as "prominent in the investigation."

The trial of my case was delayed for twelve months, but when it finally happened the brothers of the murdered nurse showed up and thanked me for my willingness to identify their sister's killer. He was sentenced to forty years for kidnapping and sent out of state to face the murder charge.

This was sobering stuff and it shook me out of my preoccupation with my own problems. I knew I didn't deserve the credit people wanted to give me for surviving the incident, but neither could I explain the way I felt about my life and the depth of my despair. "Oh, I have bad days too," people said sympathetically. Nevertheless, I had survived an ordeal and friends rallied around with support. I had a new sense of community and connectedness. But my son suffered in all of it. "Why do you have to go out running in the evening?" he would say angrily. "Don't you know it's dangerous?" "I'm fine," I'd say. "It's Burlington." He was furious. I felt like a teenager again with someone else making the rules. And here I was, young and single, and determined not to give in to fear. If only I had been able to see beyond his anger to the fear he was no doubt experiencing, we might both have fared better. I was so busy trying to cope with (or perhaps deny) my own feelings that I did not know how to acknowledge and sympathize with his anxieties. We compromised by agreeing to let each other know where we were going and when we would return, but I knew I was back in my old familiar role of resistance to authority. It was the only defense I knew.

Chapter Thirty

In the aftermath of these events, John phoned from Dublin. "Mammy has cancer," he said bluntly. "You'd better come home." I was stunned. I knew she had been waiting for a bed at the hospital for months but no one had mentioned a terminal disease. I called my women friends who promised to look after my son while I was away. Then, in a blur of mixed emotions, I flew back to Dublin and made my way to Saint Michael's Hospital in Dun Laoghaire. Mammy was in a big public ward, so I had to walk past the beds of numerous old women to reach her. The place was dripping with crucifixes and holy pictures that seemed to leap out at me accusingly. John was there and so were my sisters with small children in tow. We all gathered around Mammy in the bed except for Dad, who was sitting in a comfortable chair, eating his dinner from a hospital tray. There was Aunt May with her bright eyes with the strange brown flecks in them, sitting in another chair in the corner, her small thin-lipped mouth drawn down in a sad expression. There was a commotion at the door of the ward. Dad's relations from County Meath had arrived but they didn't want to intrude. I got up to greet them and they clustered in the doorway, patting my arm and murmuring in stage-whispers, their country accents rising and falling. Aunt Susan pressed a glass bottle into my hands. "It's Tubbernewglass water," she said, "from the holy well. It will do her good. It has a great cure for a headache." A headache. For Jesus' sake, the woman is dying of cancer, I thought, but said nothing. Dad had already warned me to say nothing, to never mention my divorce in America, to shut up about my lack of belief, to stand up when a nun entered the room.

Back at the bedside, Dad and my sister Susan were sitting on either side of Mammy, who was supported by pillows, talking in a low, halting voice but incessantly as usual. The little nun, Sister Rita, came bustling over to us, her long black habit billowing out behind her. "Oh, you have plenty of flowers," she said to Mammy. "How would you like to give some to the Church?" She picked up a bouquet that some friends had brought not five minutes before. "How would you like to give these to Our Lady?" she asked again. "Well, yes, I suppose so," Mammy mumbled, glancing from one to the other of us, seeking permission or protection, I wasn't sure which. We all looked furtively at each other, embarrassed but polite. Dad moved the bowl of blue hyacinths out of the nun's reach. He had just brought them from home and he didn't want her to rip them off. "Little hoo-er," he muttered to me as she swept out of the room. I couldn't help but laugh at his irreverence, even at a time like this.

Mammy's brother, Uncle Des, arrived in his black suit with the bicycle clips around the bottoms of his trousers. He chatted with me while Mammy was talking to someone else. "Of course, we're all on the waiting-list," he said jovially. "Once you're over seventy, anything else is a bonus. We could all be paged any day." He was right, of course, and his cheery expressions were funny in a gallows sort of way.

Underneath the chitchat, I was angry with everyone, especially Sister Rita. I even felt furious with Mammy because she had spent the past week chatting endlessly about nothing—not talking to me, not caring about me. Sometimes it was all about the details of her illness. "Did I have a good night?" she'd ask. "Am I too much trouble?" She wanted us to reassure her, tell her how good she was.

I had spent years writing cheery letters home to her and Dad, keeping them up-to-date about my son's progress, the weather, the seasons, the birds and wildlife, carefully keeping my problems to myself. It was a bit late now to let my guard down, confide in them about the kidnapping, my son's fears, my relationships, my loneliness. I had no one but myself to blame for my sense of fracture, the fault-line that seemed to run beneath the surface of my life.

Next morning Aunt Kathleen arrived, Mammy's younger and only sister and her intimate friend all her life. I watched her as she walked slowly into the ward, past the other old women in their beds. She had some minor ailment and was a patient herself in another part of the hospital. She looked solid and handsome in a man's silk dressing gown, draped over her long flannel nightie. Unlike Mammy, she had the typical Swords mane of hair, thick, wavy, and snowy white. She kissed Mammy, leaning over her, taking Mammy's face between her two hands. Then she turned away so Mammy wouldn't see her cry. I took Kathleen's hand and put my arm around her shoulders. I could feel tears welling up in my own eyes, an angry lump swelling in my throat. I was taller than Kathleen by a head, younger and stronger too, but I lacked her inner security, the simple Catholic faith of my early life.

In the afternoon the doctor made his rounds. He kept avoiding my questions, holding out hope that Mammy might recover even though she was in the fourth stage of cancer and surgery was pointless. "Oh now, you never know," he said airily. "A miracle might happen." It was his policy not to tell the patient she was dying unless she asked. Typical, I thought. Another way of fostering ignorance, childishness, the juxtaposition of the experts and the uninitiated. Just like Irish sex education—"I never told you because you didn't ask."

"It's as if they threw a handful of sand into her." This was the phrase that had been given to us by the doctor to describe the tumors in my mother's body, the phrase that was being bandied about by everyone. There was a fascination among the relatives with the gruesome details of disease. Dad, I knew, didn't want to hear about bowels and enemas. He moved away from the group of relatives and their organ recital to stand near the window that overlooked the street.

Mammy, surfacing from her dreams, mumbled of grandchildren, recipes, odds and ends. Green bile ran down the plastic tube into the bag beside her bed. "One minute she doesn't know where she is," my cousin Martin confided to me after a chat with Mammy, "the next she'll be giving you chapter and verse."

"You wouldn't want to see her become a bag of bones," said Sister

Rita when I asked what they were going to do next. I hated her for her insensitivity. This was my mother, after all. Sister Rita had a way of talking about people who were terminally ill as though they had become a different species. "Isn't it amazing how they cling to life all the same?" she would say to no one in particular. "The nurse says hearing is the last sense to go," I muttered, but Sister Rita took no notice of my remarks. Whenever Dad got his hopes up or started to feel better, she was waiting for us in the hall with some depressing update. "She's getting weaker. She won't last through the weekend."

At five o'clock Sister Rita called us into the bedside. Mammy looked awful, not human, breathing heavily like an animal, her face sunken, ghastly. Sister Rita had put a lighted candle in her hand and Rosary beads in her fingers. She began anointing Mammy with holy water and reciting the Rosary with my father. The two of them took Mammy's right hand with the candle in it and I took the other. I stared at her, transfixed by the horror of the whole situation, sickened by the religious trappings that divided me even further from her and from everyone.

Chapter Thirty-One

I was thirty-five in 1988 when Mammy died and I discovered my own gift of the gab shortly thereafter. It was then I began to write poetry in earnest and her voice that had irritated me so often began to work its lyrical magic on my inner ear. Like the swell that swept in on the tide every evening after the mailboat had crossed Scotsman's Bay, there was much to say in the silence she left behind.

After Mammy died, Dad continued to live alone in the house where we all grew up in Sallynoggin. He had purchased it from Dun Laoghaire Corporation in 1978. "Little did I think when I came up from Meath on the back of a lorry," he used to say, "that someday I would own my own house. You know," he went on, "there's a tenor I know from Wexford and every time he's asked to sing, he sings 'I Done It My Way.' That's how I feel too."

Ironically, after Mammy's death, Dad seemed to change for the better. He missed her talking and her fussing over him and the loneliness nearly drove him mad. He was forced to make friends with other people and to accept small kindnesses from the neighbors. He discovered, for the first time I think, that they were all decent people, not so very different from himself. In his eighties, he emerged as a social butterfly for whom conversation was a primary pleasure. Who knew that he—or I—had so much to say?

Ireland also experienced great changes in the late 1980s and '90s, not least of which was the referendum to legalize divorce in 1995, which was signed into law in 1996. I was amazed to discover that my parents, in opposition to the Church, had voted yes in the failed 1986 divorce referendum. "Everyone deserves a second chance," Dad said.

After I moved to America, Dad conveniently forgot that we had ever tangled. "Good girl, good girl," he would say when I called him on the phone. "There's no doubt about it," he would add, "You and John and Mary and Susan are the best four children in Ireland." I scribbled notes as we talked, doing my best to capture Dad's stories and the rhythm of his speech. Our physical resemblance was striking. The grooves beginning to etch my face from cheek to jaw were mirrors of his own. I had only to picture his face to know what mine would look like thirty years hence.

I was still far from confident when I took part in my first public poetry reading at a local bakery in Vermont. I whispered the poems apologetically, wishing the ground would open and swallow me whole. Later I plucked up the courage to enter a low-residency Master of Fine Arts program that allowed me to work full time while scribbling on the side and watching my debts increase and multiply. By the time my first poetry collection was launched several years later at the Irish Writers' Centre in Dublin, I had gained some self-assurance and had learned how to manage the talking-stick Mammy had handed me before she exited stage left for good.

So it was, after years of trying to get me out of the house when the priest came for his annual visit, and warning me not to mention my atheism or any of my other convictions in front of his relatives, Dad was immensely chuffed to be guest of honor at the book launch. Instead of his usual directive to keep my mouth shut and not be making a holy show of myself, he could say proudly, "This is my eldest daughter, the poet."

Chapter Thirty-Two

Mammy's death and the scandals that were beginning to emerge about clerical abuse in the 1990s finally prompted Dad to tell the true story about his missing eye, first to John, and later, on the phone to me in America. One day at the Technical School in Kilbride, Dad had been sitting at his desk, minding his own business, when a boy in the desk across the aisle stuck out his boot and knocked Dad's schoolbooks flying. The Master, Father Cooney, didn't bother to look into the source of the commotion, only warned Dad that if it happened again he'd be in trouble. Sure enough, the neighboring boy repeated the act and Dad was called up to the top of the classroom for punishment. Father Cooney slapped him hard across the face, shattering the optic nerve in his left eye. "I had a terrible pain in my head and I could see stars," Dad said. He was also humiliated by the incident and ashamed to tell his parents what had happened. Everyone knew it was bad luck to speak ill of a priest. Instead, he made up the story about being poked in the eye with a stick. The pain was so bad that night that his father took him on the crossbar of his bike to Navan Hospital, ten miles away, where some kind of emergency surgery was performed. Poor Dad eventually had to have the eye removed. He was heartbroken when he had to drop out of school and go up to Dublin to look for work.

Dad felt somewhat vindicated by our sense of outrage and even told his story to a Church official in Dublin. But no one ever followed up or offered compensation or an apology for what he had suffered. Suddenly so much about Dad's behavior made sense. No wonder he had been secretive and suspicious. No wonder he had wanted us to succeed where he had failed.

Dad died in 2006 on his 88th birthday. After he was gone, the world at my ear felt bereft of music. But at least I had managed to glean as much as I could before he hung up the phone forever.

After Dad's funeral, my brother and sisters and all our children went back to the house in Sallynoggin for the last time. We wandered around in little groups, taking in the meager furnishings and opening drawers to see what he had kept from his long life. Suddenly one of the grandchildren yelled, "Look what I found!" It was Dad's glass eye peering out from a small box with a plastic lid. I was horrified when everyone clustered around to stare at it. We all knew the story of the eye but this was different. It was as if we had taken this symbol of Dad's shame and put it on display at a circus sideshow. I was grateful when our John, the eldest, slipped the box into his pocket and closed the drawer. In the end, Dad deserved a little dignity and respect for what he had suffered, as well as the admiration he had longed for and coveted.

Years ago, the grassy playground at Pearse Close was filled in with concrete to make room for cars. Gone are the institutional colors of pale blue and canary yellow. Nowadays people paint their houses whatever color they choose, even adding fancy doorknockers and number-plates to the outside walls. There are no longer any children singing skipping-rhymes, faking cowboy-and-Indian death-scenes on the green, or rolling multicolored marbles into the sewers. Perhaps these things, like so much in the past, are only romantic in retrospect. But they live on in my memory, like the smell of Brompton Stock in Dad's garden, as fresh and pungent as this morning's rain.

Epilogue

Looking back at those first years in America, I can see how ill-prepared I was for life as an independent adult. My terror of driving was an obvious metaphor for my fear of growing up and occupying the driver's seat in my own life. I was raised to be polite and to please everyone, especially men, even when they turned out to be bores, bullies, or kidnappers. Growing up in the richly voluble world of Dublin in the 1950s and '60s, I had my ears out on sticks, the better to absorb the sounds and stories, words and phrases of the adults, and to crack the code of secrets that was hidden from me as a child. You could learn a lot by sitting quietly in the corner until someone noticed you and whispered that walls had ears and children should be outside in the fresh air instead of snooping around, listening to grown-up conversation. Holding my own amid the clamor of family voices was one thing, but making myself heard in the world outside was quite another. Though I rebelled against the holy trinity of my father, the Church, and misogynist Ireland, I was scared stiff once I was on my own without a male authority figure. Ironically, it was my very submissiveness, my willingness to please, and perhaps even my storytelling, that helped me survive the kidnapping incident. Afterward, an odd combination of pride, stubbornness, and curiosity kept me from completely falling apart as the years tumbled forward.

Now that I have close friends as well as a warm family, and a writing life as well as a teaching one, I can step back and look a little more tenderly at the grief-stricken young woman I used to be. Still, it does gall me when strangers seem surprised to learn that I'm Irish. "What happened to your lovely Irish accent?" they ask, as though I must be an imposter. In fact, my accent only emerges when I'm talking with my siblings, or am actually in Ireland, or talking to animals, who seem to like the sound.

What does it mean, I wonder, to lose your accent but find your voice? If my voice is the aggregate of all I have become, then I suppose it is evident in my writing if not in my speech. I began to write as a way to recall the Irish voices and turns of phrase I loved, and my work continues to be a kind of homage to all that I missed or failed to appreciate until now.

CPSIA information can be obtained at www.ICGtesting.com
Printed in the USA
BVOW08s0948260813

329390BV00007B/29/P